TRUTH FOR LIFE®

THE BIBLE-TEACHING MINISTRY OF **ALISTAIR BEGG**

The mission of Truth For Life is to teach the Bible with clarity and relevance so that unbelievers will be converted, believers will be established, and local churches will be strengthened.

Daily Program

Each day, Truth For Life distributes the Bible teaching of Alistair Begg across the U.S. and in several locations outside of the U.S. through 1,700 radio outlets. To find a radio station near you, visit **truthforlife.org/stationfinder**.

Free Teaching

The daily program, and Truth For Life's entire teaching archive of over 2,000 Bible-teaching messages, can be accessed for free online and through Truth For Life's full-feature mobile app. Download the free mobile app at **truthforlife.org/app** and listen free online at **truthforlife.org**.

At-Cost Resources

Books and full-length teaching from Alistair Begg on CD, DVD, and USB are available for purchase at cost, with no markup. Visit **truthforlife.org/store**.

Where to Begin?

If you're new to Truth For Life and would like to know where to begin listening and learning, find starting point suggestions at **truthforlife.org/firststep**. For a full list of ways to connect with Truth For Life, visit **truthforlife.org/subscribe**.

Contact Truth For Life

P.O. Box 398000 Cleveland, Ohio 44139
phone 1 (888) 588-7884   **email** letters@truthforlife.org
 /truthforlife @truthforlife truthforlife.org

"Whatever Sinclair Ferguson writes is a must-read for me. This book is no exception. Here, we find this gifted theologian at his devotional best. Every believer and family should read this clear treatment of the incarnation of the Lord Jesus Christ. Do so, and prepare to be blessed."

STEVEN J. LAWSON, President, OnePassion Ministries

"I am grateful for this book about love, as it so beautifully shows forth the redeeming love of our triune God demonstrated in the incarnation of Christ, and as it so gently directs us along the path of showing true love to our neighbor and to our sovereign and gracious Lord."

**BURK PARSONS, Senior Pastor, Saint Andrew's Chapel;
Editor, *Tabletalk* magazine**

"These devotional meditations are deeply soaked in Scripture, rich, vivid, always nourishing, sometimes challenging, often thrilling. I thank God for them."

CHRISTOPHER ASH, Writer-in-Residence, Tyndale House

"Church history will remember Dr. Ferguson as one of this generation's most insightful theological writers and biblical preachers. When you read or listen to him, you know he cares for you. And this book illumines his ability to lovingly communicate the grand themes of God's love-filled redemptive purpose."

CHRIS LARSON, President and CEO, Ligonier Ministries

"Sinclair Ferguson has written yet another book to bless and build up God's people. So read it! This devotional will warm your affections for Christ and remind you of your identity in him as a lover of God and a lover of others. Gently convicting and richly God-glorifying, this Christmas devotional is a gospel-saturated delight! Read it and celebrate the living and liberating love of God for his world."

STEVE TIMMIS, CEO, Acts29

"Amid all the glitter, goo and glow of Christmas, let *Love Came Down at Christmas* warm your heart with the wonder of God's saving purposes. Sinclair Ferguson's insightful simplicity will refresh you in the ancient Christmas story, and help you stoke the fire of devotion for God, which should characterise all our Christmas celebrations."

REV'D DR SIMON VIBERT, Vicar, Christ Church Virginia Water, UK

Love came down at Christmas,
Love all lovely, love divine;
Love was born at Christmas,
Star and angels gave the sign.

Worship we the Godhead,
Love incarnate, love divine;
Worship we our Jesus:
But wherewith for sacred sign?

Love shall be our token,
Love be yours and love be mine,
Love to God and all men,
Love for plea and gift and sign.

Christina Georgina Rossetti
(1830-1894)

Love Came Down at Christmas
© Sinclair B. Ferguson 2018.
Reprinted 2018, 2019.

Published by:
The Good Book Company

thegoodbook.com | www.thegoodbook.co.uk
thegoodbook.com.au | thegoodbook.co.nz | thegoodbook.co.in

Unless otherwise indicated, Scripture quotations are from The Holy Bible,
English Standard Version (ESV), copyright © 2001 by Crossway, a publishing
ministry of Good News Publishers. Used by permission. All rights reserved.

ISBN: 9781784982898 | Printed in the UK

Design by André Parker

CONTENTS

INTRODUCTION
CHRISTMAS IS COMING

Christmas time again and, to borrow the words of John Paul Young's song, "Love is in the air". ("Oh, oh, oh, oh, oh" was how the chorus eloquently ended, if I remember rightly.)

Love is "in the air" *every* Christmas. It features in the songs we hear as we shop for presents and in the commercials we see on TV ("Show someone they're loved this Christmas", as one department-store slogan put it). Love is present in the cards we send and in the words we write on the tags we attach to the presents we give ("With love from…").

It is a theme that is also likely to feature prominently in the annual round of Christmas interviews in the magazines and newspapers. Each year various famous people are inevitably asked what Christmas means to them. Whether they're an actor, a musician, or some sort of reality-TV "star", the answers are usually similar. "Well, it means… I wish people would just love each other. That's what Christmas is really all about, isn't it? That's what it means to me, anyway. Yes, love."

Everyone seems to agree: Christmas is about love.

As Christians, we can attest that this much is true. Christmas exists only because of love.

But what if the interviewers were to follow up by asking the "why?" and the "what?" questions? "*Why* is Christmas all about love?" and "What do you *mean* by 'love'?"

Imagine for a moment that one of the famous people they were interviewing were a Christian. It might come as a shock to the reporter if their interviewee responded to the "why?" question by saying:

> *Christmas is about love because Love came down at Christmas. That's why we have Christmas in the first place! The meaning of Christmas is found in the message of Christmas: "God so loved the world, that he gave his only Son, that whoever believes in him should not perish but have eternal life" (John 3 v 16).*

And what if the interviewee, now on a roll, continued, "And you asked me what love is, didn't you? The apostle Paul tells us in the Bible. He knew what love is because he had experienced God's love for him in Jesus. He wrote that 'The Son of God ... loved me and gave himself for me' (Galatians 2 v 20). In fact, he devoted an entire section of one of his letters to a church to explaining what love is—I remember learning it by heart a few years ago!" Can you imagine someone reciting these words?

*If I speak in the tongues of men and of angels,
but have not love, I am a noisy gong or a clanging
cymbal. And if I have prophetic powers, and
understand all mysteries and all knowledge, and if I
have all faith, so as to remove mountains, but have
not love, I am nothing. If I give away all I have, and
if I deliver up my body to be burned, but have not
love, I gain nothing.*

*Love is patient and kind; love does not envy or boast;
it is not arrogant or rude. It does not insist on its own
way; it is not irritable or resentful; it does not rejoice
at wrongdoing, but rejoices with the truth. Love bears
all things, believes all things, hopes all things, endures
all things.*

*Love never ends. As for prophecies, they will pass away;
as for tongues, they will cease; as for knowledge, it will
pass away. For we know in part and we prophesy in
part, but when the perfect comes, the partial will pass
away. When I was a child, I spoke like a child, I
thought like a child, I reasoned like a child. When I
became a man, I gave up childish ways. For now we see
in a mirror dimly, but then face to face. Now I know in
part; then I shall know fully, even as I have been fully
known. So now faith, hope, and love abide, these three;
but the greatest of these is love.*

(1 Corinthians 13 v 1-13)

The poor interviewer might be left lamely asking,
"Could you say that in just a few words?"!

In fact, you could do it in two words: Jesus Christ. He shows us what love is. Love is simply being like him.

So, love is a lot more than just having good feelings about someone else. It is the greatest thing in the world, but it is also the most demanding.

The Christian faith has a grammar all of its own. If we mess up the grammar of a language, we will not be able to speak it properly. In the grammar of the Christian faith, what we are called to be and do is rooted in who God is and what he has done for us in Christ. So the resources we need to love others are found in the love of Jesus Christ for us. That is why, when we read Paul's words, we need to keep our ears open for echoes of Jesus' life and look for his shadow falling on every line.

So, before you begin to read this book—which is all about 1 Corinthians 13—take a few moments to read that passage, preferably out loud (it was originally written to be read that way). When you come to the second paragraph, wherever you see the word "love" or "it", substitute your own name. See how far you get!

Then, read the chapter again. But this time, in the same second paragraph, when you see "love" or "it" substitute the name "Jesus"—and read to the end.

These two ways of reading the passage go together. The first tells us what we are called to be as Christians— and exposes how far short we have fallen. The second tells us what Jesus is like.

In the days leading up to Christmas, we are going to walk through this passage line by line and explore what it means for us.

"Why choose this passage for Advent?" one might ask. 1 Corinthians 13 is among the best-known chapters in the Bible. Quotations from it or references to it appear in some unexpected places. Bob Dylan alluded to it in his song "Dignity" released in 1994. Prince Charles read it at Diana's funeral service in 1997. President Obama referred to it in his first inaugural speech in 2009. Perhaps no words have been read more frequently at wedding services than these.

But when you slow them down, and read them phrase by phrase, and apply them to yourself, they transpose into a different key altogether. They cease to be rhetorically pleasing and emotionally soothing; instead they become an analysis of your spiritual life. They are deeply challenging.

Perhaps that's not what we expect at Christmas time. But the real meaning of the Christmas story is challenging as well as heart-warming. It is about love coming down. And it makes us think about love in a new way.

So, let's take a deep breath and begin to explore how and why *Love came down at Christmas*—and the difference this makes to our lives.

1. OF MEN AND ANGELS

If I speak in the tongues of men and of angels,
but have not love,
I am a noisy gong or a clanging cymbal.

1 Corinthians 13 v 1

Angels are in fashion—at least at Christmas time!
Look at any collection of hymns or songs, and
you may well find more references to angels in the section marked "Advent" than in all the other sections
added together.

The New Testament word for "angel" means a messenger. Every time angels appear in the Christmas story,
they are carrying messages from heaven to earth.

In the run-up to Jesus' birth, angels appeared to
Zechariah, the father of John the Baptist, to Mary, the
mother of Jesus, and—in dreams—to Joseph, his adop-
tive father (like his Old Testament namesake, Joseph
was a dreamer). A vast crowd of them appeared to a
few shepherds in the fields outside Bethlehem. Interest-
ingly, it's clear that all these angels spoke the local language—which happens to have been Aramaic, a form
of Hebrew. Angels can speak in human tongues.

So, what does Paul mean when he begins the "love chapter" (1 Corinthians 13) with a reference to angel tongues as well as human tongues?

This isn't the first time Paul has talked about tongues in this letter to the Corinthians. In the previous chapter, he writes about their ability to speak in "various kinds of tongues" (12 v 10). In the next chapter he devotes 28 verses to discussing these tongues (14 v 1-28). Clearly this was a big deal in Corinth. Whether these "tongues" refer to foreign languages or ecstatic speech, the Corinthians—or at least some of them—may have believed they could speak "Angel". Presumably speaking "Angel" carried more kudos than any other language. Imagine being able to speak the language of heaven! Were some of them even claiming that they had spoken with angels?

When one of our grandsons was about eight or nine, he told me how excited he was to be going to France for his summer holiday "because I'll be able to practise my French on the French!" I said nothing. Despite five (miserable!) years studying French in school, I was silently thinking, "The French are the *last people* on whom I would want to practise my French"—and in my experience they have always agreed with me. But being able to practise your French on the French is nothing compared to being able to practise "Angel" on angels! Imagine it today: a publisher would offer a ghostwriter if need be to get your story. You'd be on the bestseller list and interviewed on TV ("Tonight we meet the author of *I Spoke with Angels*—this year's number one bestseller").

But notice what Paul says: if you can speak "Angel" but you lack love, you are "a noisy gong or a clanging cymbal". You may think you're special, but in God's eyes—and ears!—you act and sound like a brass instrument making a loud, unpleasant noise. Actually, he doesn't say, *You sound like.* He says, *You are.* You are not what you think you are.

Metalworking was a significant industry in first-century Corinth. So, the Corinthians knew all about what Paul meant. Imagine a little Corinthian factory where the craftsmen made gongs and cymbals! All that clanging and banging—the Berlin Philharmonic it wasn't! You would want to cover your ears with your noise-reducing headphones. That's what speaking in tongues sounds like in God's ears if the speaker lacks love.

Some scholars think Paul may have been thinking about the metallic amplification systems that were crafted in Corinth for use in the theatre: *You think you are something? You are just a self-amplifier!*

You probably don't claim to have the ability to speak "Angel". But what Paul seems to be doing here is applying a general principle to a specific problem he saw in Corinth. That problem keeps on recurring. You encounter it whenever you meet someone who wants to tell you all about his or her gift (or "gifting", as people like to say today). Ministers and pastors are sometimes asked, "If I become a member of your church, will I get to use *my gift*?" "Will my gifts be *recognised* by the church?" Or even, "Why aren't my gifts being recognised by this church?"

Paul valued the gifts of the Spirit, but he wasn't much interested in that approach. His first question at a church-membership interview would not be about your gifts. He'd want to know about your love—about how you want to serve others for Jesus' sake. He'd "sound you out"—perhaps in more than one sense! He knew that any true fellowship of God's people will make room for our gifts when people see we want to serve others because we have come to love them.

Isn't it odd that this chapter about love, which so many people "love", begins by telling us what love isn't? And about who doesn't have it? Not really. One of the best ways of explaining something is by saying what it isn't. Paul often does that. It helps eliminate a great deal of wrong thinking and misunderstanding. Here he says that *love isn't the same thing as having great gifts.* You might be a very gifted teacher. You may be applauded as a musician. You might be admired for your spiritual prayers. But none of that matters if you do not love.

But if 1 Corinthians 13 contains a description of love, it must ultimately be a description of Jesus. And Jesus did speak with the tongues of angels as well as of men.

Jesus not only spoke "Angel"; he spoke *with* angels (Mark 1 v 13; Luke 22 v 43). He is their King. They are his servants and ambassadors. Throughout his earthly life they were—appropriately enough—waiting "in the wings" to do his will. Even on the cross he could have summoned legions of them and they would have come immediately to rescue him (Matthew 26 v 53). But he knew he couldn't rescue us if they came to rescue him.

It was him or us who would be saved, and he chose us. Although he could speak with the tongues of angels, he remained silent—because he loved us so much. Instead he spoke to his Father and asked him to save those who were watching him ("Father, forgive them," he prayed). That was more important to him than speaking to the angels and asking them to save him.

In fact, Jesus not only spoke angel-language. He spoke the language of God: "In the beginning was the Word, and the Word was *with* God" (John 1 v 1). He was face to face with God, in intimate conversation with his Father. But "the Word became flesh and dwelt among us" (v 14). He came face to face with us, taking our nature so that he might speak to us. As the Nicene Creed, an ancient statement of faith, affirms, "For us and for our salvation he came down".

Whatever gifts you may have, love always means that you come down. It means that you use those gifts for the good of others, not to make yourself feel good. It means that you are willing to do things that are uncomfortable or inconvenient for you, or that go unnoticed.

For "If I speak in the tongues of men and of angels but have not love, I am a noisy gong or a clanging cymbal". If so, I am not like Jesus. And ultimately, love is being like Jesus. It silences all noisy gongs, clanging cymbals and self-amplification systems. Real love always comes down. We know that because *Love came down at Christmas*.

REFLECTION

Are you more concerned with using your gifts, or with loving others? How could you use your gifts in service of others this week?

PRAYER

Love through me, Love of God;
There is no love in me.
O Fire of love, light thou the love
That burns perpetually.

Flow through me, Peace of God;
Calm River, flow until
No wind can blow, no current stir
A ripple of self-will.

Shine through me, Joy of God;
Make me like thy clear air
That thou dost pour thy colours through,
As though it were not there.

O blessed Love of God,
That all may taste and see
How good thou art, once more I pray:
Love through me—even me.

> *Amy Carmichael (1867-1951)*

2. GLITTERING POWERS

*And if I have prophetic powers, and understand all
mysteries and all knowledge, and if I have all faith, so
as to remove mountains, but have not love,
I am nothing.*

1 Corinthians 13 v 2

The popular press allows you to consult your horoscope, but Bible prophecy is firmly out of fashion. Except, that is, at Christmas time. Even if a Service of Lessons and Carols combines readings from Charles Dickens and the like with the book of Genesis, the prophet Isaiah is still there. You can't have a real Christmas service without prophecy. It's an essential part of the story. In fact, Matthew's account of the birth of Jesus is held together by a whole series of prophecies about his coming (Matthew 1 v 22; 2 v 6, 15, 18).

One of the remarkable things about these prophecies is that the baby Jesus could not have engineered their fulfilment. The point is that, through the prophets, God had foretold what would happen.

True, most Old Testament prophecy isn't like that. It's not so much *fore-telling* the future as *forth-telling* God's word for the present. Perhaps that is why Paul links it here with understanding what he calls "mysteries" (by which he doesn't mean spooky things, but things we can't understand unless God explains them to us). But in either sense, being able to prophesy was also a big deal in Corinth. It was a prominent spiritual gift. Paul seems to have valued it above all the other gifts, even speaking in tongues (1 Corinthians 14 v 1). But a loveless prophet is "nothing".

As if that were not enough, Paul adds something else: mountain-moving-faith without love is also nothing. He probably knew Jesus had spoken about this kind of faith (Matthew 17 v 20; Mark 11 v 23). We still use the expression "faith that moves mountains". It is picture language. None of the apostles moved mountains to make their journeys easier; they went the long way around, or even by sea. Moving mountains means doing what seems impossible.

Likewise, the word "faith" here doesn't mean simply "trusting Jesus". You can't be a Christian without that kind of faith. But Paul is speaking about a special gift that not everyone had (he had explained this earlier in 1 Corinthians 12 v 8-10, 29-30). Mountain-moving faith—like making a lame beggar walk or the blind see—is extra-ordinary.

Our instinct is to be in awe of a person who can prophesy or who has mountain-moving faith. We tend to assume that anyone who can do those things must be deeply spiritual, and marked out for a position of leadership and for a "ministry" that we should support, perhaps even financially.

But there is a problem. Apparently, you can have mountain-moving faith and not have love. And if that's true, instead of being someone to be respected, followed and supported—you're nothing. That's no thing; nobody; zero.

You should keep a careful watch on people who claim to have special gifts. In particular, you need to watch their lifestyle. You can't afford to be naïve. And most of all you need to avoid the biggest mistake—confusing gifts with grace. They are not the same. Having special gifts, even extraordinary ones, is not a mark of grace.

Does that sound like sour grapes on the part of somebody who doesn't have mountain-moving faith? It could be. But the fact is, it is what Jesus himself said:

> *On that day many will say to me, "Lord, Lord, did we not prophesy in your name, and cast out demons in your name, and do many mighty works in your name?" And then I will declare to them, "I never knew you; depart from me, you workers of lawlessness."* (Matthew 7 v 22-23)

These words are from Jesus' Sermon on the Mount, a passage that has something in common with 1 Corinthians 13: everybody loves it, but not everybody hears what it's saying.

So, what is the point? This: when Christ gives you a gift, it will be a blessing to you; but the gift isn't primarily for you. It is to enable you to express your love for him by serving others. Paul had these gifts in abundance. But whenever he used them he would say, *We are your servants (bond-slaves) for Jesus' sake* (for example, see 2 Corinthians 4 v 5).

You may have met people who complain, "The church isn't recognising my gifting". But you probably have never heard anyone complain, "The church isn't recognising my *loving*"! The truth is that if we are focused on looking for opportunities to love, we'll usually find opportunities to use our gifts along the way.

The Holy Spirit accompanied Jesus throughout the whole course of his life, from the moment of his conception until his resurrection (Luke 1 v 35; Romans 1 v 4). Throughout his life he had the Holy Spirit "without measure" (John 3 v 34). In the face of all the pride and failure of his little disciple band, he never said, *You're not recognising my gifting.* Instead...

> *Jesus, knowing that the Father had given all things*
> *into his hands, and that he had come from God ...*
> *rose from supper. He laid aside his outer garments,*
> *and taking a towel, tied it round his waist. Then*
> *he poured water into a basin and began to wash the*
> *disciples' feet and to wipe them with the towel that was*
> *wrapped around him.* (John 13 v 3-5)

Jesus had all prophetic powers; he understood all mysteries and all knowledge. He had mountain-moving faith. But because he loved us, he kept coming down. See him in the upper room, kneeling at the feet of his sinful disciples. Since Judas didn't leave the room until later on (v 30), we know that Jesus *knelt down and washed the feet of his betrayer.*

We see this humble love in its perfect form at the first Christmas. The incarnation means that "though he was in the form of God … [Christ] made himself nothing, taking the form of a servant, being born in the likeness of men" (Philippians 2 v 5-8). That is what love looks like. That is what love is. And that *Love came down at Christmas.*

REFLECTION

"The church isn't recognising my gift!" Have you ever felt something similar? What will you seek to remind yourself of next time that happens?

PRAYER

I ask thee for a thoughtful love,
Through constant watching wise,
To meet the glad with joyful smiles,
And to wipe the weeping eyes;
And a heart at leisure from itself,
To soothe and sympathise …

Wherever in the world I am,
In whatsoe'er estate,
I have a fellowship with hearts
To keep and cultivate;
And a work of lowly love to do
For the Lord on whom I wait.

So I ask thee for the daily strength,
To none that ask denied,
And a mind to blend with outward life
While keeping at thy side;
Content to fill a little space,
If thou be glorified ...

In a service which thy will appoints
There are no bonds for me,
For my inmost heart is taught "the truth"
That makes thy children "free";
And a life of self-renouncing love
Is a life of liberty.

Anna Laetitia Waring (1820-1910)

3. THE DEAD GIVEAWAY

*If I give away all I have, and if I deliver up my body
to be burned, but have not love, I gain nothing.*

1 Corinthians 13 v 3

I was in my early teens when I became a Christian. In those days "sacrifice" was a big word. When my Bible class teacher gave away some of his books, the one I received was *Sacrifice* by Howard Guinness.

And then there was Elisabeth Elliot's book *The Shadow of the Almighty*, written about the sacrificial life of her husband, Jim, who was killed by the Auca (Huaorani) people of Ecuador. I once had the privilege of speaking at a conference with her, and telling her that when I was a teenager I knew more or less by heart whole sections of her book. Everybody knew the oft-quoted words from his journal: "He is no fool who gives what he cannot keep to gain what he cannot lose".

I remember as a teenager hearing Gladys Aylward speak about the sufferings of young Christians in China—willing to sacrifice their lives for the Lord Jesus.

Before that there was C.T. Studd, the English cricketer who played in the match against Australia that was the origin of "the Ashes", and who later became the founder of the Worldwide Evangelisation Crusade. He wrote a challenging little tract about professing Christians being "chocolate soldiers" rather than real ones (they melt if things get hot!).

And there was Amy Carmichael, whose little book *If* was a compilation of sayings that all began "If I…" and ended "… then I know nothing of Calvary love". The message was that if sacrifice wasn't at the heart of your life, then you would "know nothing of Calvary love".

Sacrifice. I lost count of the number of sermons and talks I heard in those days about taking up the cross to follow Jesus, about counting the cost, about not turning back, about giving everything to Christ.

But something must have changed since then. These days I hardly ever hear a message or see a book that majors on sacrifice. Am I getting old and blind and deaf—or is it really the case that "satisfaction" seems to have replaced "sacrifice" in our vocabulary?

Perhaps this explains why we can gloss over these words of Paul about giving everything away and even our body being burned. At least in the West, you're not likely to have to give your body to be burned—like the Scottish martyrs Patrick Hamilton, burned to death in St Andrews on 29 February 1528, and George Wishart, likewise on 1 March 1546. Or like the English bishops Hugh Latimer and Nicholas Ridley on 16 October 1555, or Archbishop Thomas Cranmer on 21 March 1556. You can still go to the spots where these horrific events took place. But you're not likely to experience them yourself. Others maybe; elsewhere perhaps. But not where we live. Is that why Paul's words do not seem to scratch where we itch?

But martyrdom isn't the first thing Paul mentions here to make his point. He begins with giving all your possessions away—the very thing the rich young ruler in the Gospels couldn't bring himself to do. He simply had too many of them to let go (Matthew 19 v 16-24). Maybe this comes closer to home. What if Jesus asked you to do that?

A friend told me about a memorable experience at a student conference. One of the leaders read out the words of Frances Ridley Havergal's hymn "Take my life, and let it be". He invited the students to respond to each line with a hearty "Yes!" It went something like this:

Take my life, and let it be consecrated, Lord, to thee... —*Yes!*

Take my moments and my days; let them flow in ceaseless praise... —*Yes!*

Take my hands, and let them move at the impulse of thy love... —*Yes!*

Take my feet, and let them be swift and beautiful for thee... —*Yes!*

Take my voice, and let me sing always, only, for my King... —*Yes!*

Take my lips, and let them be filled with messages from thee... —*Yes!*

*Take my silver and my gold; not a mite would I
withhold…*

Silence.

The students had the integrity to realise that at this
point professions of love for Christ might be measurable.
They were not, apparently, sure they loved the Lord Jesus
enough to impoverish themselves for him. At that point
enthusiastic response became self-revealing silence.

By contrast, Paul had been impoverished for Christ.
For Christ's sake he had "suffered the loss of all things".
Perhaps he had been disinherited. But in any case,
he counted all things as "rubbish" (the word means
"dung") by comparison with Christ (Philippians 3 v 8).
And he was willing to die for Christ. But here he was
telling the Corinthians that it is possible to "suffer the
loss of all things" (including one's life in excruciating
circumstances) and yet "gain nothing" if love is lacking—love for Jesus that produces love for others.

The message is shocking; but it is basically simple. The
motives and intentions of our hearts can be very devious.
We can make great sacrifices, and yet do so grudgingly
rather than lovingly. We can fall into the subtle trap of
thinking the sacrifice itself impresses God.

You'll probably be invited, or expected, to give generously of your money and time in some way this Christmas—perhaps at church or at home. But amid all the
busyness, the message of Christmas brings us back to
first principles. It shows us what love is. And the first
principle is this: Jesus gave everything he had, because

he loved us. He gave his body to the cross because he loved us. Before that he lived his life in a loveless world because he loved us. But first of all he came because he loved us. The Creator became part of his creation; the Lord of glory came to this fallen earth, to take upon himself the consequences of the sin of the world.

Why did he come? Because he loved us. Why did he die? Because he loved us. Why did he love us? Because he loved us.

If we lose sight of that, we will never love him properly. Perhaps we will never be able to love anybody properly. For until we have tasted his love, we can never fully appreciate why love makes us willing to sacrifice everything.

If we are going to live lovingly as well as sacrificially, we must look at the One who did both.

REFLECTION

In what area of your life do you feel that you are (or ought to be) making a sacrifice? How has what you have read today challenged your attitude in that area?

PRAYER

Let your love so warm our souls, O Lord,
that we may gladly surrender ourselves with all that
we are and have to you.
Let your love fall as fire from heaven
upon the altar of our hearts;
teach us to guard it carefully

by continual devotion and quietness of mind,
and to cherish with anxious care
every spark of its holy flame,
with which your good Spirit would quicken us,
so that neither height nor depth,
things present nor things to come,
may ever separate us therefrom.
Strengthen our souls, animate our cold hearts
with your warmth and tenderness,
that we may no more live as in a dream,
but walk before you as pilgrims
in earnest to reach their home.
And grant us all at last to meet with your holy saints
before your throne,
and there rejoice in your love.

Gerhard Tersteegen (1697-1769)

4. ANYONE FOR PATIENCE?

Love is patient.

1 Corinthians 13 v 4

A colleague once told me about a very embarrassing experience. He had flown out of town for a speaking engagement. The flights were badly delayed and so he arrived at his hotel very late and exhausted. The young man at the reception desk asked for his name, looked for his reservation, and after a few minutes said, apologetically, "I'm sorry sir, but there's no record of a reservation in your name".

It was the straw that broke the camel's back. More pointedly, it destroyed the theologian's patience—he flew off the handle.

Eventually the young receptionist found him a room and asked my friend to sign the paperwork. He wrote his name, and then the address of the (well-known!) theological seminary where he taught. The young man looked on in amazement and gasped, awestruck: "You're really Professor _____ from _____ Seminary? I just became a Christian a few months ago. What a privilege to meet you!"

It can happen to the best of us! Something makes us snap. Later, we protest in embarrassment, "I don't know what came over me. I'm usually very patient!".

But that's not true. It is just that we have never really been tested. Only impatience-stimulating situations show whether we are patient or not! The Christmas season will present plenty of opportunities to test our patience: packed trains, traffic jams, crowded shops, orders we made on websites arriving too late—or without batteries—not to mention difficult relatives or over-excited children!

In the course of his teaching on love, Paul now turns from negative to positive characteristics of love. It's interesting—don't you think?—that he begins with patience.

The English word "patience" can be used to translate several different words in the Greek New Testament. Paul's verb here (*makrothumeō*) means "to be long-tempered". He seems to have associated this with humility and gentleness (Ephesians 4 v 1-2; Colossians 3 v 12). It shows itself in the way Christians "bear with" one another.

The Bible contains some great examples. A quarter of the book of Genesis is devoted to describing how God developed patience in one man. The story begins with a naïve and impatient seventeen-year-old boy who then experiences fourteen years of suffering, injustice, and disappointments. As a result, he learns humble trust in God. But then it turns out that these long years of painful training have prepared him to exercise the kind of patience that will be needed to negotiate the following fourteen years as Prime Minister of Egypt. Now he has the wisdom to manage seven years of bumper harvests in order to cope with seven years of famine.

The young man's name was, of course, Joseph, and his story is told in wonderful detail in Genesis 37 – 50. The end result? His brothers come to Egypt and eventually discover who he is. The whole family is reunited with him. But when their father dies, his brothers fear that his kindness has been only temporary, and that his apparent longsuffering has been simply a slow building up of a head of steam that will propel his revenge. They do not need to fear, because Joseph has in fact learned to be patient, gentle, and longsuffering. He has learned how to love.

What is the explanation? His brothers "meant evil" against him. But he knew that "'God meant it for good, to bring it about that many people should be kept alive, as they are today' … Thus he comforted them and spoke kindly to them" (Genesis 50 v 20-21).

Joseph's story is like a movie version of Romans 8 v 28: "We know that for those who love God all things work together for good". God has ways and means of making everything work for good for his people. He has a purpose for their lives. When you know this, it builds longsuffering into you.

The secret to this kind of patience doesn't lie in natural disposition. There's a weakness to be found somewhere inside you, even if you haven't yet discovered it. Some of us seem to be amazingly patient with big things but then we fly off the handle at the trivial ones.

But love is always patient, always longsuffering. It can be patient in difficult situations because it knows God has a plan. It can be patient with difficult people because it knows they are God's image (Genesis 1 v 26).

Love is not a commodity that comes down from heaven waiting to be unwrapped. No—it is actively exercising patience with other people and with the circumstances God has ordained. It is being able to take the long-term view, knowing that nothing can happen to us without the will of our heavenly Father. Love acts and reacts without tensing up in irritation because life isn't fair, without blaming other people for what we are experiencing, and without planning how we'll get even.

Have you ever wondered about these words in Charles Wesley's Christmas hymn "Hark! The herald angels sing"?

Late in time behold him come,
Offspring of a virgin's womb.

Was Wesley complaining that Jesus was too late— that he might have (should have?) come earlier? That would be a misunderstanding of Wesley. He knew well enough that Jesus was born "when the fullness of time had come" (Galatians 4 v 4). But, as the phrase "late in time" indicates, it was after centuries of preparation.

What does that say about the Son of God, who became flesh? He was patient. He waited, as it were, until all was ready—when David's royal line had reached perhaps its lowest point, in the home of a Nazareth carpenter and a teenage mother.

The child in the manger is the perfect example of divine patience. The rest of his life gave expression to it. How longsuffering he was. He experienced opposition, virtually from the moment he stepped into the world. Later he tasted misunderstanding in his own family, who didn't trust him. And then those disciples—so often foolish, at the most critical juncture in his life, they disappointed him. "Have I been with you so long, and you still do not know me?" Jesus asked Philip (John 14 v 9). "Could you not watch one hour?" he asked Peter, James and John (Mark 14 v 37).

And then, on top of it all, there was betrayal by a man who had broken bread with him a matter of hours before—then an illegal trial, false witnesses, a judge with no moral fibre, a wrongful conviction. And then the spitting, the abuse, the humiliation, and the shame and agony of the cross.

If you want to know what patience is, what longsuffering looks like, all you need to do is to read through one of the Gospels. Yes, "love is patient". Jesus was patient. And if the Lord of loving patience lives in you, your love will be patient too.

But there's more. For if you think about it, the greatest illustration you know of his longsuffering is the way he has been so longsuffering towards you.

REFLECTION

Who or what has tested your patience in the past few days? How did you respond? How do you imagine Christ would have responded if he were in your shoes?

PRAYER

Whate'er you, Lord, ordain is right:
Your holy will abides;
I will be still whate'er you do;
And follow where you guide;
You are my God; though dark my road,
You hold me that I shall not fall:
Wherefore to you I leave it all.

Whate'er you, Lord, ordain is right:
You never will deceive me;
You lead me by the proper path:
I know you will not leave me.
I take, content, what you have sent;
Your hand can turn my griefs away,
And patiently I wait your day.

Whate'er you, Lord, ordain is right:
Here shall my stand be taken;
Though sorrow, need, or death be mine,
Yet I am not forsaken.
My Father's care is round me there;
You hold me that I shall not fall:
And so to you I leave it all.

Samuel Rodigast (1649-1708), altered.

5. THE MILK OF HUMAN KINDNESS

Love is ... kind.

1 Corinthians 13 v 4

This verse, apparently, is the first time that the Greek verb "to be kind" has been used in any written work still in existence. Kindness existed. It's just that writers don't seem to have used the verb "to be kind". It is almost as if the whole of Greek literature were saying: *We can define what kindness is, but we have never really seen it in action—until now.*

Augustine of Hippo wrote at the end of the fourth century that he was sure he knew what time was—until he was asked! Perhaps we feel the same about kindness. We are sure we know exactly what it is until someone asks us to define it! Then it seems to run into a whole series of other qualities. Kindness is being caring, thoughtful, gentle, treating others better than they deserve; it is generosity; kindness is ...

One thing kindness is not: it is not spectacular. It isn't showy.

Do you know how important one man's kindness was to Augustine? He has proved to be one of the most significant thinkers in the history of the Christian church. You could fill a room with books and articles written about his thinking.

Augustine's spiritual pilgrimage is fascinating. His Christian mother prayed fervently for her gifted son. But he was determined to do things his own way. He tried everything going, but his final judgment on the experiment makes him sound like a member of the Rolling Stones, lamenting, "I can't get no satisfaction" (although if Augustine had written in English, he would have probably avoided the self-cancelling double negative!). When you read his life story, you can readily imagine him adding, "And I've tried, and I've tried, and I've tried…"

So, what do you think it would take to bring this brilliant but prodigal son, hard-wired to achieve fame, into the kingdom of God? One of the people who influenced him was a man internationally renowned for his oratory—the very thing Augustine craved. His name was Ambrose. He was Bishop of Milan.

"Of course," we might instinctively think, "it would take a superstar to make an impact on someone who wants to be a superstar". But what drove the eloquence of Ambrose was the gospel. At first Augustine listened to him thinking he could overlook the substance for the sake of his style. It took a little time for him to realise that in the case of Ambrose the style was actually the fruit of the substance.

Looking back, years after he had become a Christian, Augustine tells us what happened:

I came to Milan, to Ambrose the Bishop ... It was by you [Lord] that, unconsciously, I was led to him so that by him I might consciously be brought to you! That man of God received me like a father; when I came he showed me the kindness of a bishop. From that point I found myself beginning to love him. But at first it was not because he was a teacher of the truth—I had no expectation that I would find that in your Church! It was because he was kind to me personally. I listened carefully to him when he preached to his congregation, not as I should have done, but instead assessing his eloquence to see if he really merited his reputation ... and yet little by little I was drawing near, quite unconsciously.

Ambrose was a superstar preacher. But notice what Augustine said made the significant impact on him and caused his opposition to Christ to begin to melt. The solvent? Ambrose "was kind to me personally".

You probably don't have the gifts of an Ambrose. And perhaps you would find meeting someone as intellectually gifted as Augustine a little intimidating. Few of us feel we have the brain power to persuade somebody like that to become a Christian. But it isn't brain power that draws people to Christ. That isn't what first drew Augustine to Christ. It was kindness. And that—as Augustine eventually discovered—is just another way of saying that Ambrose was like Jesus—because Jesus is kind. Love always is.

Tucked away in his little letter to his colleague Titus, Paul gives a unique description of what happened at the incarnation: "The ... loving kindness of God our Saviour appeared" (Titus 3 v 4). Augustine caught a glimpse of that in Ambrose before he realised it was Jesus he was seeing reflected in the good bishop.

Jesus was kind to the poor and the needy but also to the rich and unsatisfied; he was kind to little children—they trusted him and allowed him to pick them up; he was kind to parents who had lost their twelve-year-old daughter; to a woman who had suffered from blood loss during the same twelve years; to a widow whose son had died; to a tax collector who had feathered his own bed by profiteering; and to an uber-confident disciple who kept messing up and saying and doing the wrong things. And then he was kind to a young man named Saul who thought he could mastermind the destruction of the entire Christian church. On the road to Damascus, Saul (soon to become Paul) discovered the real identity of Jesus—that he was the one through whom "the ... loving kindness of God our Saviour appeared".

And, yes, he has been kind to you as well, hasn't he?

So, Christmas is about love appearing in the form of kindness. The kind Son of God took our flesh, shared our nature, expressed his love for us, and died our death. And when he rose he was no less kind. He has been kind to us in our sin and need. That kindness is intended "to lead you to repentance" says Paul (Romans 2 v 4). That is what it did to Saul of Tarsus. It was what it did to Augustine when he caught a glimpse of it in Ambrose. Perhaps you also saw that kindness in someone, and it has drawn you to the love of Christ.

One final, and obvious, thought. You don't need to be important, wealthy, well-educated, brilliant, famous, or eloquent to help point people to the Lord Jesus. All you need to do is to be kind to them with the loving kindness of Jesus. And Christmas gives us plenty of opportunities to do that. Being kind is how love works. The Holy Spirit takes care of the rest.

REFLECTION
Reflect on some ways in which you have tasted God's loving kindness. Who could you seek to show the loving kindness of Jesus to today?

PRAYER
Ah, Lord, dost thou not see my heart?
Alas, how little love!
I pray thee, do not lose thy part;
Drop softness from above.
Oh, keep it tender, keep it soft,
That I may know to raise,
And quickly fit the lowest string,
Unto a tune of praise.

Make my heart softer, softer still,
Me like thy mourning dove;
I mourn because I cannot mourn,

Sinclair B. Ferguson

But Lord, thou knowest I love.
Make my heart softer, softer still,
That by thy gracious hand,
A deep impression may be made,
Even from the least command.

John Mason (1646-1694)

6. HAPPY WITH YOUR LOT

Love does not envy.

1 Corinthians 13 v 4

Does this seem odd to you? Sometimes we find it difficult to love people precisely because they are so obviously loved by others. What is the reason? The green-eyed monster. It doesn't begin as a monster, but as a little flea. Small though it is, its bite gets under the skin. It makes us itch, and then we scratch and it gets worse. Inflammation results and infection sets in. Before you know it, the poison is in your whole system. At its worst, this little green-eyed monster can be fatal.

In fact, envy led to the crucifixion of Jesus. Of course, there was more to it than that, but not less. Even Pontius Pilate "knew that it was *out of envy* that [the religious leaders] had delivered [Jesus] up" (Matthew 27 v 18; compare Mark 15 v 10). "Delivered up" is the verb that is used regularly in the New Testament for Jesus' judicial condemnation. Envy crucified Jesus. It is a lethal poison.

Is there an antidote for envy, even a cure? Yes—love.

Paul is back to negatives again: he lists behaviour patterns that love never exhibits. Perhaps that is because the things love *doesn't do* were the very things the Corinthians were doing.

For starters, love "does not envy". Paul had already mentioned the Corinthians' jealousy back in 1 Corinthians 3 v 3. Now in chapter 13 he seems to suggest that you can have some of the greatest gifts in the world and yet be a walking reservoir of envy. You may even cultivate it, but envy is not your friend. It makes your bones rot (Proverbs 14 v 30); and it leaves a bitter taste (James 3 v 14).

"True," you might say, "but envy and jealousy would not be allowed room in a church like ours". Well, Christians in Rome and the dispersed Christians to whom James wrote all needed to be warned against it (Romans 13 v 13; James 3 v 14, 16).

So, are you jealous of somebody? Does reading that question bring a name or face to mind? Is this what is spoiling your relationship with them? Has it got to the stage where you can't think of, and you struggle to say, anything positive about them? And when their name comes up in conversation, do you instinctively say something negative about them? Just enough to take the glitter off their reputation? Or, because you want to *appear* nice, do you admit their qualities but then qualify them with a "But…" that pulls them down and expresses the envy in your heart?

Of course, Christmas can present a whole new set of reasons to be envious. Perhaps this time of year brings into sharp focus the families at church who are better off than yours; or the friend's husband who buys more thoughtful gifts than yours does; or the colleagues who can afford yet another skiing holiday over New Year.

Have you any idea of the spiritual damage that envy is doing to you? Of course not. But the green-eyed monster is gradually turning you into someone who can never be content. You will always be grasping to have someone else's position or reputation—always wanting to have what God has given to someone else. So long as that is true, you will never be able to say:

> *I have learned in whatever situation I am to be*
> *content. I know how to be brought low, and I know*
> *how to abound. In any and every circumstance, I*
> *have learned the secret of facing plenty and hunger,*
> *abundance and need. I can do all things through him*
> *who strengthens me.*   *(Philippians 4 v 11-13)*

This is a far cry from our own jealous mindsets. In fact, to speak as Paul does here seems almost impossible. So how can envy for someone else be transformed into contentment with our own life? Love is the solution.

The basic meaning of the Greek verb "to love" (*agapaō*) was "to be happy with your lot". The Greek philosopher Plato used it this way in *Lysis* (his work on friendship): "I was as joyful as a hunter, completely happy (*agapētos*) to have at last the very thing I was pursuing".

Jesus is the great example, isn't he? No trace of jealousy in him. Why was that? Why is there no sense with

Jesus that he felt or thought or said, "I deserve better"? A little earlier in his letter to the Philippians, Paul gives us the answer.

> *Christ Jesus … though he was in the form of God,*
> *did not count equality with God a thing to be grasped,*
> *but made himself nothing, taking the form of a*
> *servant.*　　　　　　　　　　　　　*(2 v 5-7)*

Here Paul tells us what was going on inside Jesus' mind, what he was thinking. But that isn't all Paul wrote. We missed out his introductory words. Usually Paul gives exposition and then his exhortation. But here he begins with an exhortation and then explains its foundation:

> *Do nothing from rivalry or conceit … Let each of you*
> *look not only to his own interests, but also to the*
> *interests of others. Have this mind among yourselves,*
> which is yours in Christ Jesus.　　　　　*(2 v 3-5)*

Notice his logic:

- As Christian believers you are united to Christ ("in Christ" is how Paul usually puts it)
- Because of this you have the "mind … which is yours in Christ Jesus"
- Therefore, show the mind of Christ in your lives.

Later on in the same chapter he describes two men, Timothy and Epaphroditus, who illustrated the mind of Christ. They shared Christ's disposition and put others first. They loved them. This is the antidote for envy.

The sin of jealousy can be traced all the way back to Cain, and beyond that to Eden, and perhaps beyond that to Satan himself, in his envy of the King of the angels, God's Son. The evil one found a way of introducing his own disposition into our DNA. But there *is* a cure, and it's found in the love of God in Christ—as Germanus of Constantinople wrote in his carol:

> *A great and mighty wonder,*
> *A full and holy cure!*
> *The virgin bears the Infant*
> *With virgin-honour pure.*
> *Repeat the song again!*
> *"To God on high be glory,*
> *And peace on earth to men!"*

Christ is the remedy for our envy. The cure was given when *Love came down at Christmas.*

REFLECTION

Who are you tempted to envy? What would it look like for you to show the mind of Christ instead?

PRAYER

> *Lord, my heart is before you.*
> *I try, but I myself can do nothing; do what I cannot.*
> *Admit me into the inner room of your love.*
>
> *I ask, I seek, I knock.*
> *You have made me ask; make me receive.*

You have enabled me to seek; enable me to find.
You have taught me to knock; open to my knock ...

I faint with hunger for your love; refresh me with it.

Let me be
filled with your love,
rich in your affection,
completely held in your care.
Take me and possess me wholly,
who with the Father and the Holy Spirit
are alone blessed from age to age.

Anselm of Canterbury (1033-1109)

7. ONE GREAT MYSTERY

Love does not ... boast.

1 Corinthians 13 v 4

The Authorised (King James) Version of the Bible sounds so much more eloquent than modern versions when it translates these words as "Charity vaunteth not itself". But the words themselves describe something malevolent.

When Paul says "Love does not ... boast", the verb he uses appears only here in the New Testament. It means to grow large but without substance; put more brutally—to be a wind-bag. It is a verb often associated with the use of words, either spoken or written. Of course, the development of social media now enables us to boast in picture form too.

We sometimes speak about people who are "all style and no substance". A friend I was visiting gave me a recording of a sermon to listen to while he ran an errand. He was interested to know what I thought of it. He knew what he was doing. I listened for ten minutes and could bear it no longer. The voice was magnificent, the presentation dramatic, the pronunciation perfect—but in ten minutes the preacher had said—nothing. There was wordiness and eloquence, but there was no weight; it was all too "showy". Whatever words were used, the subliminal message seemed to be "See how eloquent I am!" But love (and preaching should always be an expression of love for those who are listening) does not draw attention to itself. It deliberately seeks to follow the way of humility—and not in order to show how humble it is!

Why is love never like that? Because of something that is basic to becoming a Christian.

Simon Garfield's book *Mauve* has a subtitle that prepares us for the story it tells: *How One Man Invented a Colour That Changed the World*. In the mid-nineteenth century the colour-dyeing of materials was a painstaking and expensive process. Garfield tells us that the garments used in one royal procession in the nineteenth century required the death of ten million insects!

But all that changed in 1856 when William Perkin, an eighteen-year-old chemist, was working on a treatment for malaria in his little home laboratory, and "accidentally" made a dark oily sludge (instead of artificial quinine!). But it turned out that this sludge could turn silk into a beautiful light purple—mauve.

It soon became the most sought-after shade in the fashion houses of London and Paris, and earned Perkin both a fortune and a knighthood. He turned chemistry into a technology—the *Tribune* wrote that his feat would remain unequalled until the time came when chemists found a way of making artificial food!

Sir William Perkin was a Christian. When he was on his deathbed someone said to him, "Sir William, you will soon hear the 'Well done, good and faithful servant'". In response he said, "The children are in Sunday School. Give them my love, and tell them always to trust Jesus." He then began to recite Isaac Watts' hymn "Crucifixion to the world by the death of Christ":

> *When I survey the wondrous cross*
> *On which the Prince of glory died,*
> *My richest gain I count but loss,*
> *And pour contempt on all my pride.*

Reaching the last line, he commented quietly, "Proud? Who could be proud?"

How can a man be empty of pride when he has revolutionised an industry, been honoured by his queen, and made a fortune? You need to know something about yourself that is bigger than anything you have achieved or ever could. Sir William knew what that was. It created an atmosphere so rich and dense that it asphyxiated pride. It creates humility, a disposition that is deeper than modesty. What is it? The love of Jesus Christ for us. It causes what the nineteenth-century Scottish minister Thomas Chalmers called "the expulsive power of a new affection". It creates in us a love for Christ and then for others.

When John's Gospel tells us that "God so loved the world, that he gave his only Son, that whoever believes in him should not perish but have eternal life" (John 3 v 16), it combines two truths in one sentence.

First, God gave his Son to us when Christ came into the womb of a virgin and emerged from it as a new-born infant. He came to share our humanity from its beginning—as an embryo cradled in the body of a teen-aged virgin. Who can measure the distance between the brightness of the throne of glory and the darkness of the womb of Mary? This mystery is the wonder of the incarnation.

But that is not the only sense of the verb "gave" in John 3 v 16, as becomes clear in the context. The Father who gave his Son *to us* in the incarnation also gave him *for us* at Calvary. That is how God proves his love for us—when we were weak and helpless, sinners and enemies, he gave his Son to die for us (Romans 5 v 6-10). This mystery is the wonder of the crucifixion.

Together these constitute the one great mystery of the gospel: that the Son of God came down "for us and for our salvation". And in the presence of this mystery pride is asphyxiated.

Proud? Who could be proud?

There is no room for boasting, except in this: *Love came down at Christmas.*

REFLECTION

What is it about the incarnation and crucifixion that asphyxiates pride? In what particular areas do you need to ask for God's help to banish boasting?

PRAYER

Come down, O love divine,
Seek thou this soul of mine,
And visit it with thine own ardour glowing.
O Comforter, draw near, within my heart appear,
And kindle it, thy holy flame bestowing.

Let holy charity
Mine outward vesture be,
And lowliness become mine inner clothing;
True lowliness of heart, which takes the humbler part,
And o'er its own shortcomings weeps with loathing.

And so the yearning strong,
With which the soul will long,
Shall far outpass the power of human telling;
For none can guess its grace, till he become the place
Wherein the Holy Spirit makes his dwelling.

Bianco da Siena (1350-1399)

8. HARMONIOUS HUMILITY

Love … is not arrogant.

1 Corinthians 13 v 4

Those who love do not entertain over-inflated views of their own importance and demean others in the process. They are not arrogant. They are not like the woman of substance in Edinburgh who, after hearing a sermon on humility preached by the Presbyterian minister Alexander Moody-Stuart, said to him, "You don't preach nearly enough on the subject of humility, Mr Moody-Stuart. And that's a pity, because *humility is my forte!*"

Do we need yet another negative from Paul—another description of what love is *not*? Today "negativity" is almost always seen as bad. But the positive cannot survive unless you are also negative about the negative!

This principle is broadly applicable. It is true in learning. We are helped to learn what something is partly by understanding what it is not. It is also true in medical diagnosis. If you are sick, you go to the doctor and tell him your symptoms. In the process of diagnosis, your doctor will go through a process of elimination, deciding what the problem is *not*. Elimination narrows the field of possibilities and in that way has a "positive" effect.

The same is true in the New Testament. It is a hugely positive book—none more so. But have you ever counted the number of negative things Jesus said? Or the number of times Paul says, essentially, *You need to be negative [here] if you are going to be positive [there]*?

So, Paul is laying the groundwork for helping us to understand what love is by explaining what it *isn't*. If you think about it, you will see that the Law of God worked in the same way. Hidden in each of God's negatives (and most of the commandments are negative) lies a positive.

What, then, does Paul mean when he says that love is "not arrogant"? Is he hinting that the Corinthians were? It is always a good idea to read Scripture in context (words in their verses, verses in their chapters, chapters in their books, books in their Testament and so on). When we do that here, we discover that Paul has already given some clues about what he means.

Paul was concerned that arrogance was revealing itself in the Corinthian church in the way some of them were "puffed up in favour of one against another" (1 Corinthians 4 v 6). There were groups within the church—perhaps even separate little house churches—who were ranking their preachers, and in the process setting themselves up as superior. One group favoured Paul, with his great learning and amazing conversion story. Another gave the prize to Simon Peter, with his eyewitness stories about Jesus (plus he had that "fragility" that some people liked. His earlier life was punctuated with failures; for example, Matthew 16 v 22-23; 26 v 69-75; Galatians 2 v 11-14). Others were impressed by Apollos, who appears to have been more eloquent than either of the others (Acts 18 v 24-28).

A friend was preaching in a local church during an annual Christian convention. As he wrote his name and text in the church book, he leafed through the entries from previous years to see which convention speakers had preceded him. He noticed something unusual: little marks beside their names. Slowly it dawned on him: the local incumbent had been grading the preachers!

We all do it; or almost all of us. I remember cringing inwardly for a minister I knew when—in his presence—his wife announced to me the name of her favourite preacher. You've guessed it: it was not her husband! Of course, apart from possibly one wife in the world, preacher's wives all must listen to the world's second-best preacher. But it must be a heavy burden to know your wife sits listening to you scores and more times a year when someone else is her "favourite"! In his providence, God may equip one preacher or another to be especially helpful to us. Yet isn't there something immature about ranking them—or for that matter doing the same thing with other members of the church because of the gifts God has given them? God measures us by how much we grow in grace, not by the position we occupy because of our gifts.

Ranking Christians and their gifts was a hobby among the Corinthians. They were doing it with preachers, and they were doing it with each other. The arrogance behind it was a deep-seated problem. Paul said it was carnal, not spiritual. They were forgetting that they had received *charismata*—grace gifts, love gifts. Each gift was given by the same Jesus. Whether it was preaching or serving, each was brought to them by one and the same Holy Spirit (1 Corinthians 12 v 4, 11). And all of them were God's gifts. So ultimately it was the Lord's work they were ranking!

Paul "goes on" about this in his letter (see 4 v 18-19; 5 v 2). At one point he focuses his sights on an area in which the Corinthians regard themselves as superior— their "knowledge" (8 v 1). But "this 'knowledge' puffs up" (he uses the same verb as in 13 v 4). By contrast "love builds up".

Here, then, is a significant insight for us. What can deliver us from being "puffed up" in relation to our fellow Christians? Not having an inflated sense of our own ego helps. So does realising how sinful pride is.

But Paul tells us there is a more powerful remedy yet. It is recognising that whatever gift I have comes from the same Lord Jesus as the gifts of every Christian in the church family. So "who sees anything different in you? What do you have that you did not receive? If then you received it, why do you boast as if you did not receive it?" (4 v 7).

Why, then, is love not arrogant? What produces the harmony between giftedness and humility? The incarnation shows us the way:

> *For you know the grace of our Lord Jesus Christ, that*
> *though he was rich, yet for your sake he became poor,*
> *so that you by his poverty might become rich.*
> *(2 Corinthians 8 v 9)*

Our Lord Jesus Christ exchanged the throne of glory for a manger borrowed from animals; when he was presented in the temple, his parents could afford only the offering made by the poor (Luke 2 v 22-24; see Leviticus 12 v 6-8). He had no place to lay his head; his only possession of any worth when he died was a seamless robe someone had lovingly made for him; he was buried in a borrowed grave. Yes, he became poor to make us rich. No wonder then that Paul wrote:

> *[Therefore] do nothing from rivalry or conceit, but in*
> *humility count others more significant than yourselves.*
> *Let each of you look not only to his own interests, but*
> *also to the interests of others. Have this mind among*
> *yourselves, which is yours in Christ Jesus, who, though*
> *he was in the form of God … made himself nothing,*
> *taking the form of a servant … and … humbled*
> *himself.*   *(Philippians 2 v 3-8)*

There is no room for arrogance when every gift we have is from Jesus. Paul teaches us that humility replaces arrogance when we see that *Love came down at Christmas.*

REFLECTION

What gifts have you been given by Jesus? Remember what he gave up to give them to you. How will that move you to humbly love others today?

PRAYER

May the mind of Christ, my Saviour,
Live in me from day to day,
By His love and power controlling
All I do and say.

May the Word of God dwell richly
In my heart from hour to hour,
So that all may see I triumph
Only through his power.

May the love of Jesus fill me
As the waters fill the sea;
Him exalting, self abasing,
This is victory.

May I run the race before me,
Strong and brave to face the foe,
Looking only unto Jesus
As I onward go.

May His beauty rest upon me,
As I seek the lost to win,
And may they forget the channel,
Seeing only him.

Kate Barclay Wilkinson (1859-1928)

9. LOVE HAS GOOD MANNERS

Love ... is not ... rude.

1 Corinthians 13 v 4-5

An intriguing article appeared last year in one of the major "quality" newspapers in the United Kingdom. The theme of the op-ed piece by the "progressive" journalist was that now—in the new moral order—life was so much better. His comments stuck in my memory banks. There is indeed so much about life that is better today: advances in science, medicine, communications, the availability of education, decent standards of living and so on. But none of these is related to recent "progress" in our moral or religious habits. In that area, unlike the journalist, I question the "progress".

The article was sufficiently memorable (or irritating?) that in the following weeks I regularly scanned the same newspaper's headlines. They constituted a catalogue of almost unmitigated sorrow, crime, and crises, much of it caused by what our culture used to call "sin". The headlines seemed to say, *Better? Not according to this paper!*

One of these headlines appeared a couple of days after the article that initially stirred my interest. It was another op-ed piece; but this time the author was not a journalist but a stand-up comedian. Not being an expert in this genre, I had vaguely assumed that being rude in one form or another, even if playfully, was part of a stand-up comedian's stock-in-trade. To my surprise (and perhaps rebuke!) the theme of the article was "Have you noticed that there seems to be so much more rudeness today?" The contrast between the articles struck me as significant. Is there a link between the jettisoning of Christianity in our culture and an apparent increase in rudeness? Is there a kind of inevitability about this?

If love is not rude, the implication of Paul's words is that rudeness springs from the absence of love.

We need to probe this a little. Secular attacks on biblical norms are almost always based on the notion that Christianity is a myth. The popular notion is that once we have rid ourselves of the influence of the myth, we will all get back to being the decent, loving, tolerant, justice-seeking human beings we were before Christianity invaded and "destroyed" our cultures. This is forgetting that prior to the coming of the Christian faith, Western culture was a form of paganism.

What, then, is lost when we lose our Christian world view? Our highest dignity—that as men and women we have been made as the image of God, created specifically for loving fellowship with him and with each other (Genesis 1 v 26-28). When we demean God, we inevitably do the same to his image—one another.

Disconnected from the love of God and from loving him, the foundation and motivation for respect begins to crumble. There is a kind of inevitability that rudeness will result—to God and man.

Thankfully, in God's common grace the remnants of love remain. But the positive impact made on society by the gospel is being drained away. The stand-up comedian seemed perplexed as to why being rude has become "cool". But the answer is that when we deliberately seek to eliminate the God of the gospel from communal and personal life, we must needs suffer the consequences in small as well as in big things. That is Paul's point in Romans 1 v 28-32:

> *And since they did not see fit to acknowledge God, God gave them up to a debased mind to do what ought not to be done. They were filled with all manner of unrighteousness, evil, covetousness, malice. They are full of envy, murder, strife, deceit, maliciousness. They are gossips, slanderers, haters of God, insolent, haughty, boastful, inventors of evil, disobedient to parents, foolish, faithless, heartless, ruthless. Though they know God's decree that those who practice such things deserve to die, they not only do them but give approval to those who practise them.*

All that adds up to rudeness and much more. But in 1 Corinthians 13, Paul is teaching us the antidote. The gospel reaches into and transforms the small details of our lives as well as its overall direction.

J.B. Phillips' translation expresses Paul's words positively: "Love has good manners". What do you make of that? Good manners? A rather Victorian thought? Is it important for "millennial" Christians to have good manners? Or has J.B. Phillips simply given us a translation that would appeal only to some elderly churchgoers in the 1950s? Are "good manners" at best only quaint? Would it be "not cool" to have them?

I once witnessed a memorable illustration of the effect of gospel love on manners. Just as a crowded meeting in our church fellowship hall was about to begin, a very elderly man entered the room. There were no vacant seats. Virtually every man in the room stood up simultaneously to offer him any seat he wanted! Fuddy-duddy? Perhaps. But has it ever struck you that the New Testament says that love is the fulfilling of the law (Romans 13 v 10)? What then does that love *look like*? What if the answer is "It looks like fulfilling these words from the law: 'You shall stand up before the grey head and honour the face of an old man'" (Leviticus 19 v 32). It makes you think!

Christians are not rude. That negative implies a positive: they are polite, respectful, caring, thoughtful, well-mannered. That doesn't mean they are slaves of social etiquette, but lovers of biblical etiquette! Read through your New Testament and mark every verse that describes the Christian's lifestyle. You will discover that Christians are called to have deeply countercultural manners—such different manners that others can't help noticing, and wondering why! Or try this: read through the Gospels and see what good manners Love Incarnate had. He was never rude or said "smart" things just to get a laugh. Here's how he is described in the pages of the Bible:

> *My servant ... will not quarrel or cry aloud, nor will anyone hear his voice in the streets;*
> *a bruised reed he will not break, and a smouldering wick he will not quench.*
> *(Matthew 12 v 18-20, quoting Isaiah 42 v 1-3)*

> *All ... marvelled at the gracious words that were coming from his mouth.*   *(Luke 4 v 22)*

> *I am gentle and lowly in heart.*   *(Matthew 11 v 29)*

Paul tells us that the sending of Christ into the world was the first of two sendings: the Father who sent his Son also sends the Spirit of his Son into the hearts of believers (Galatians 4 v 6). The Spirit who indwells the Christian is none other than the Spirit who dwelt in the incarnate Son. He is not another, different Spirit, but one and the same Spirit of Christ. He indwells us to make us more like the Lord Jesus, who was conceived in the womb of his mother, Mary, and was born in Bethlehem—and he was never, ever rude.

So, "do not grieve the Holy Spirit of God, by whom you were sealed for the day of redemption" (Ephesians 4 v 30). Remember each day that love is not rude; it never does anything unseemly. This is the lifestyle that points people to the Lord Jesus. It is what we will pray

for this Christmas when we sing Edward Caswall's carol,
"See Amid the Winter's Snow":

Teach, O teach us, holy Child,
By thy face so meek and mild,
Teach us to resemble thee,
In thy sweet humility.

REFLECTION

"Christians are ... well-mannered." Does that thought
surprise you? How do you think biblical etiquette differs
from social etiquette?

PRAYER

Light of Light, and God of God,
who did bow your holy heavens
and come down to earth for the salvation of the world,
out of your love of humanity;
extend your almighty right hand, and send out your
blessings on us all ...
Guide our steps in the paths of righteousness,
that we may behave ourselves according to your will
and observe your commandments
and do them all the days of our life
and come to a blessed end and sing a ceaseless hymn
with your saints
to you, and your Father, and your Holy Spirit.
                    Dioscorus of Alexandria (died 454)

10. THROW YOURSELF IN

Love ... does not insist on its own way.

1 Corinthians 13 v 4-5

In our culture we are obsessed with one thing: ourselves. In the absence of any transcendent significance to life, creating, loving, and fulfilling the self fills the vacuum. Youngsters are taught from a very early stage—often in schools—to trust in themselves, to know that they are princesses and princes, and to be assured that they can do anything to which they set their minds.

It is perhaps not surprising that in an age when secular scientists insist we are exclusively material beings, and tell us that there is no "self" other than our biological functions, the longing to find a self has taken on epidemic proportions. People can "self-identify" as this or that. Thus self-directed love is seen as the fundamental birthright—even while our governments take it upon themselves to decide when there is a self who has the right to birth.

The problem—as Augustine saw so clearly—is that *amor sui* (self-directed love) leads to personal and societal disaster whenever it is severed from *amor Dei* (God-directed love).

Of course, there is a proper love of self. Jesus said we should love our neighbour as ourselves—so the implication is that we will love the latter too. But why is that not the same as self-love? Because it isn't self-directed love. Instead, it is rooted in realising that since we are made as the image of God, we should treat his image with respect and care—and we should do the same to others, who likewise are the image of God.

The secular humanist, who denies that humans were created as the image of God, thus makes man out to be far less than he is seen to be in Christian teaching. In fact, Christians are the higher humanists; secularists by comparison are de-humanists and reduce the dignity of man.

Yet, despite it all, men and women remain the image of God, and inevitably they thirst for significance even although they cannot explain why. So long as that is the case, Augustine's most famous words remain true: God has made us for himself (we are his image) and our hearts are therefore restless until they find their rest in him.

But left to ourselves, all we have is ourselves. Indeed, as some secularists have had the courage to say, in this worldview there simply is no meaning to life; there are no answers to what have always been thought to be the ultimate questions:

- Why is there something and not nothing?
- Who am I?

- What is the purpose of life?
- What is my destiny?

If we have to invent our own answers to these questions, it is hardly surprising that *amor sui* is promoted so vigorously. Yet the questions cannot be suppressed, even when we repress them. Is there no answer to them? Perhaps Lily in Jane Wagner's play, *The Search for Intelligent Life in the Universe*, is right when she says:

I worry where tonight fits in the cosmic scheme of things.

And then she adds:

I worry there is no cosmic scheme to things.

Christmas says there is a cosmic scheme of things. God made us as his image to reflect his glory. We have sinned and fallen short of that glory (Romans 3 v 23). But the Son of God, who is the very image of God (Colossians 1 v 15), was sent by God, and came in love to restore his image. Through faith in him, we discover that our lives fit into "the cosmic scheme of things". He recreates in us a love for himself and restores us to fellowship with himself, which transforms self-directed love into love of our neighbours. That is the destiny for which we were created.

In this way the birth of Christ leads to our rebirth (John 1 v 9-13). That new birth sets us free from the tyranny of the project of the self. In Christ we enter a "new creation", where life begins to make ultimate sense (2 Corinthians 5 v 17). And since we have found our true identity in Christ, we are no longer left to our own devices to try to discover who we really are.

Here is a neat little summary of what happened at that first Christmas from the early fathers of the Christian church: "Christ became what he was not in order that we might become what we were not". In order to fill us, the Son of God emptied himself; and in order to give us life, the Son of God became obedient to death, even death on a cross (Philippians 2 v 5-11). And when we trust him, we too die to self and begin to live for him and for others. For he died "that those who live might no longer live for themselves but for him who for their sake died and was raised". This, says Paul, takes place when "the love of Christ controls us" (2 Corinthians 5 v 14-15).

The incarnation of the Son of God was a radical event. And the gospel is a radical message. Jesus said that the discovery of self always involves losing or denying self (Luke 9 v 24). And what does denying ourselves look like? Often, it looks like not insisting on our own way when we could, and instead laying down our preferences for the sake of others. Sometimes that means that we won't insist on celebrating Christmas with that particular part of the family or in this particular way or with those particular traditions. We won't insist that we're too tired to help with the washing up. Instead we will choose to love—and "love … does not insist on its own way".

In George MacDonald's fantasy tale *The Golden Key*, one of the characters, Tangle, meets the Old Man of the Earth, who gives her further directions in her life-quest:

> *Then the Old Man of the Earth stooped over the*
> *floor of the cave, raised a huge stone from it, and left*
> *it leaning. It disclosed a great hole that went plumb-*
> *down.*
> *"That is the way," he said.*
> *"But there are no stairs."*
> *"You must throw yourself in. There is no other way."*

The discovery of who we were created to be takes place in the same way. There are no stairs; you need to throw yourself into the love of Christ. It is an all-or-nothing thing. In trusting him, you will lose your life, but at the same time, you will find it. You must die to self to find yourself. And then you will be set free from the self-love that has crippled you all your life. But you must first "throw yourself in. There is no other way."

Jesus said that there is only one way to the Father— himself (John 14 v 6). And the fact that he came at Christmas means that you can throw yourself into loving selflessly today.

REFLECTION

"You need to throw yourself into the love of Christ." What holds you back from that? What would "throwing yourself into" selfless love look like for you today?

PRAYER

O Love that wilt not let me go,
I rest my weary soul in thee;
I give thee back the life I owe,
That in thine ocean depths its flow
May richer, fuller be.

O light that followest all my way,
I yield my flickering torch to thee;
My heart restores its borrowed ray,
That in thy sunshine's blaze its day
May brighter, fairer be.

O Joy that seekest me through pain,
I cannot close my heart to thee;
I trace the rainbow through the rain,
And feel the promise is not vain,
That morn shall tearless be.

O Cross that liftest up my head,
I dare not ask to fly from thee;
I lay in dust life's glory dead,
And from the ground there blossoms red
Life that shall endless be.

George Matheson (1842-1906)

11. EASILY IRRITATED?

Love ... is not irritable.

1 Corinthians 13 v 4-5

It is easy to get irritated at Christmas time with the overplayed Christmas jingles that miss its real meaning, or the impossible-to-untangle Christmas-tree lights (whose fault is it?), or the "Look how well *our* children are doing" Christmas letters. At one level the causes of our irritation seem obvious enough. But a deeper irritation usually goes unrecognised—irritation with God.

A minister I knew sometimes took an unusual pastoral approach with people. He would ask them to read through the parables of Jesus and tell him which ones irritated them! I think he was on to something.

Preachers are often told that what really helps people is narrative—stories. That was how Jesus preached. He told parables.

Maybe it is true that stories help people understand better. But that is not why Jesus told parables. In fact, he said that he told them to make clear who *didn't* understand them (Matthew 13 v 10-15)! They might like the story but entirely miss its point.

My friend was much nearer the mark. Jesus' parables are meant to get under our skin, to reveal that our sin has created within us an irritation with God and his ways. And until we embrace Christ in the gospel, we will continue to be irritated with God and refuse to yield to him.

Take the parable about the Pharisee and the tax collector in Luke 18 v 10-14:

> *Two men went up into the temple to pray, one a Pharisee and the other a tax collector.*
>
> *The Pharisee, standing by himself, prayed thus: "God, I thank you that I am not like other men, extortioners, unjust, adulterers, or even like this tax collector. I fast twice a week; I give tithes of all that I get."*
>
> *But the tax collector, standing far off, would not even lift up his eyes to heaven, but beat his breast, saying, "God, be merciful to me, a sinner!"*
>
> *[Jesus added] "I tell you, this man [the tax collector] went down to his house justified, rather than the other."*

Of course! You knew that. But that is only because you are familiar with Jesus' punchline to the story. And if you're honest, that line no longer has any "punch" for you—which may mean you still don't get it. For the people who listened to Jesus, his words must have felt like a blow to the stomach. But if you think honestly about it, you will notice something. You may in fact be more like the Pharisee than the tax collector!

The chances are you go to church, so for a start you are "not like other men". You thank God for keeping you from sin, don't you? Plus, you have high moral standards—you try not to cheat, you treat people fairly, you are not sexually immoral like so many other people. And you engage in religious activities; you try to give faithfully, and to be disciplined. And it is a long time since you beat your breast in church (even metaphorically) and cried out for mercy. Maybe you once beat your breast. But now—well, you don't see so much need for that these days—not now that you've been forgiven.

So, are you more like the Pharisee than the tax collector? If so, here's the problem: it was the tax collector who walked out of the temple justified. God's ways in this parable can be just as irritating to us as in Jesus' parable about equal pay for labourers in a vineyard no matter how many hours in the day they had worked. It can be very irritating to discover that "the last will be first, and the first last" (Matthew 20 v 1-16).

But what is the point of this diversion into understanding the parables? Simply this: only when this fundamental irritation is brought to the surface and dealt with by God's grace will we begin to experience and express the love that "is not irritable".

Irritation with God and his ways was injected into the human race in the Garden of Eden. *Don't you see that God isn't really fair and loving?* said the serpent. *Did he surround you with fruit-bearing trees just to irritate you by not letting you eat of any of them?* Eve struggled a little, but her vision was already beginning to be distorted (Genesis 3 v 1-7). That irritation with God soon became irritation between husband and wife, and then brother and brother (Genesis 3 v 12; 4 v 3-8).

If we are going to be delivered from being irritable, we need to find a cure for this fundamental irritation with God about his ways. Only then will we be able to love and not be irritated.

Irritability—by whatever name we call it, and whether caused by other people or our circumstances—is at root irritation with God for the way he is providentially governing our lives. We blame our circumstances, or other people, or our background, or even our genes—but none of these can function apart from God's sovereign will and purpose! Only when we have yielded to the sovereign will of God, knowing that he will work everything together for our good, do we learn a healthy spiritual detachment from the irritations of life.

That doesn't mean we are fatalistic. It does not mean that we do not try to change things for the better, relieve pain or remove obstacles to happiness. But now we do all those things with our hearts at rest in God, knowing that he works for the good of those who love him (Romans 8 v 28). The remedy for my irritability, therefore, will not be found in a determination to be less irritable, but only in a sense of the love of God for me, and in the trust in him it produces.

Jesus' life was marked by irritants from beginning to end. From birth in an outhouse to followers who proved to be fickle, enemies who plotted against him, people who disappointed him, religious leaders who planned to kill him, an empire whose representative declined to vindicate him, soldiers who vented their cynicism upon him, spectators who came to watch his crucifixion—his whole life was one long saga of irritants. Yet we hear no irritable word (Isaiah 53 v 7; 1 Peter 2 v 22-23); we see no irritated action or reaction. What we observe is a humble bowing before his Father's will.

How was that possible? Because he loved his Father, trusted his plan, and knew that his ways were perfect. When he comes to indwell us by his Spirit, that same grace in which he lived from the womb to the throne begins to be reproduced in us.

There was no irritability in Jesus. In fact, it was to deal with ours that *Love came down at Christmas*.

REFLECTION

Think about some specific irritations that you feel. Can you identify the irritation with God at their root? How does what you've read today counter that attitude?

PRAYER

Make me a captive, Lord,
And then I shall be free.
Force me to render up my sword,
And I shall conqueror be.
I sink in life's alarms
When by myself I stand;

Imprison me within thine arms,
And strong shall be my hand.

My heart is weak and poor
Until it master find;
It has no spring of action sure,
It varies with the wind.
It cannot freely move
Till thou hast wrought its chain;
Enslave it with thy matchless love,
And deathless it shall reign.

My power is faint and low
Till I have learned to serve;
It lacks the needed fire to glow,
It lacks the breeze to nerve.
It cannot drive the world
Until itself be driven;
Its flag can only be unfurled
When thou shalt breathe from heaven.

My will is not my own
Till thou hast made it thine;
If it would reach a monarch's throne,
It must its crown resign.
It only stands unbent
Amid the clashing strife,
When on thy bosom it has leant,
And found in thee its life.

George Matheson (1842-1906)

12. THE FATHER'S HEART

Love is ... not ... resentful.

1 Corinthians 13 v 4-5

Have you ever encountered someone like this? Their memory-retrieval system staggers you. Something is said, or done, and immediately they recall a comment you made six months or even a year ago. They bring it up, throw it back at you, and it seems—at least in their own estimation—they now re-establish their dominant position. It can really spoil your Christmas!

I recall a friend making a comment about a particular situation when—with lightning speed—something he had said over a year earlier was thrown back in his face in an accusatory spirit. It was as though his accuser had been waiting eighteen months for just the right moment to use his words against him. This is not the sign of a great memory, or of high intelligence, but of a resentful spirit.

There is something satanic about an ability to keep a mental dated index of rights and wrongs done. It is a form of self-love, always either defending or aggrandising itself. It is not even necessary for the person resented to be known personally, but only that they have a reputation that can be resented. That resentment—like jealousy—may appear in subtle and thinly disguised ways.

The name of someone especially gifted or well known is mentioned with appreciation. Resentment rears its ugly head in response by pointing out some fault or failing or deviation from "our" norms. Or it simply adds a piece of gossip about the other person so that his or her reputation is destroyed. And not infrequently this is accomplished under the guise of piety. The resentful heart cannot bear not to be superior.

Such people often take what they see as the moral high ground to buttress their words.

Think of Judas Iscariot. Remember when Mary of Bethany anointed Jesus' feet with a huge quantity of expensive ointment and then wiped them with her own hair (John 12 v 1-7). Judas simply could not hide his resentment. He had already calculated the value of the perfume at an entire year's salary. What a waste! It could have been sold (*should have been sold!*) and the money given to the poor. It would have done so much good! But John exposes Judas's resentful heart. He was the treasurer of the disciple band, and was embezzling the finances. He had probably already calculated the amount he could safely cream off the proceeds, "because he was a thief".

This Judas-like spirit is often disguised as spirituality. But it hides a sinful heart, hostile to Christ. The question "What most honours and glorifies the Lord Jesus and demonstrates love for and gratitude to him?" never entered Judas's resentment-filled head.

Love—for the Lord Jesus and for others—means that you delight to see someone expressing honour, love and devotion to them. But resentment simply cannot stand wholehearted, unselfconscious, spontaneous displays of love for Christ. It can hardly bear to watch.

In addition, resentment is always making calculations. In fact, Paul uses an accountancy metaphor here. Love does not calculate, make a tally of, or reckon up grudges. Resentment always does. It creates an entire bank account of them. It waits for the right opportunity. Then it acts. In particular it cannot remain inactive in the presence of generous love.

But think about this: no one ever had more justification for resentment than the Lord Jesus. But he did not come into the world to settle a score. Instead, his generous love led to the sacrifice that covers all our sins and has the power to dissolve our resentment.

But first we need to be persuaded that he does love us. A little chorus we used to sing as youngsters says it all:

He did not come to judge the world.
He did not come to blame.
He did not only come to seek,
It was to save he came.
And when we call him "Saviour"
And when we call him "Saviour"
And when we call him "Saviour"
We call him by his name.

We know that Jesus did not come to blame. But some Christians live with a paralysing fear that the Father still harbours a spirit of blame towards them. After all, didn't Jesus need to die to persuade his Father to forgive us? Doesn't that suggest a certain reluctance on the Father's part?

Sometimes the gospel is preached in these terms: "Because Christ died for you, the Father now loves you". But this is profoundly muddle-headed. The truth is a diameter removed.

Jesus did not die to persuade the Father to love us. It was *because* the Father loved us that he sent Jesus to die for us. How much we need to see and feel the implications of this: "God [the Father] so loved the world, that he gave his only Son … God did not send his Son into the world to condemn the world, but in order that the world might be saved through him" (John 3 v 16-17). What Jesus said to the apostles in the upper room he says to all his disciples: "The Father himself loves you" (16 v 27). There is nothing un-Jesus-like in God; there is no hidden resentment in his heart towards his children.

Without this conviction it is likely that the spirit of resentment will continue to lie deep within our hearts. That is why it is so important to appreciate that it is the Father's love, and the Father's initiative, that lies behind the incarnation:

In this the love of God was made manifest among us, that God sent his only Son into the world, so that we might live through him. In this is love, not that we

have loved God but that he loved us and sent his Son
to be the propitiation for our sins.   (1 John 4 v 9-10)

Notice that in these verses "God" is a reference to God the *Father*—who sent his Son. Yes, the Son became incarnate because he loved us. But in his coming the Father's *Love came down at Christmas*.

REFLECTION

In what ways do you struggle with a spirit of resentment? Are you ever tempted to think that the Father resents loving you? What is the link between these two attitudes?

PRAYER

O God, the light of every heart that sees thee,
the Life of every soul that loves thee,
the strength of every mind that seeks thee,
grant me ever to continue steadfast in thy holy love.
Be thou the joy of my heart;
take it all to thyself, and therein abide.

The house of my soul is, I confess, too narrow for thee;
do thou enlarge it, that thou mayest enter in;
it is ruinous, but do thou repair it.
It has that within which must offend thine eyes;
I confess and know it;
but whose help shall I implore in cleansing it,
but thine alone?
To thee, therefore, I cry urgently,

begging that thou wilt cleanse me from my secret faults,
and keep thy servant from presumptuous sins,
that they never get dominion over me. Amen.
                    Augustine of Hippo (354-430)

13. REJOICING: RIGHT OR WRONG?

*Love … does not rejoice at wrongdoing but rejoices
with the truth.*

1 Corinthians 13 v 4-6

I once heard of a Christian student group who reproduced and distributed in booklet form Paul's words
in Romans 1 v 18 – 3 v 20 without indicating their
source. In these verses Paul powerfully and relentlessly
exposes the sinfulness of all humanity and argues that
we are guilty before the judgment seat of God. Soon
the student leaders were required to appear before the
university authorities because of the inflammatory nature of the literature they were distributing. They were
also told to bring the author!

It was a very revealing incident. The academic authorities, apparently, had no knowledge of Paul's letter to the
Romans, despite its status as probably the most famous
and certainly the most studied letter ever written and the
manifesto of Christian faith. Not only so, but by their
reaction they were unwittingly giving testimony to its

continued relevance. Paul's exposé of sin ranges from creature worship, through shameless and unnatural sexual relations, to parental disobedience and ruthlessness.

The closing words of Romans chapter 1 are particularly telling: "Though they know God's decree that those who practise such things deserve to die, *they not only do them but give approval to those who practise them*" (Romans 1 v 32). It's sometimes said that misery needs company—and it turns out that sin and sinners do too. Other people must be encouraged to share the sinful lifestyle, for numbers provide validation and justification—after all, if everyone else is doing it, it must be OK. That's why sin will not rest content with toleration of its presence; it demands "approval" and eventually celebration. We see that in our culture now more than ever.

And in the face of such sin, we might conclude that all the Bible's talk about the "wrath of God" is an empty threat. No thunderbolts come from the heavens in response! But what Paul makes clear is that God's present expression of his wrath is that he gives people over to their own desires (v 24, 26, 28). The effect is that what they rejoice in is self-destructive. As C.S. Lewis notes, the words "Thy will be done" can be the most terrible in the universe, if spoken by God himself.

Christian love moves in a very different direction. It does not rejoice in sin and its consequences but in God and his grace—in beauty, in goodness, and in truth (Philippians 4 v 8).

Why is rejoicing with the truth and not in wrongdoing so important? Because, one way or another, we tend to become like whatever we rejoice in. And that cannot remain hidden.

Many years ago, as I wrote (or better, *scrawled*) on a book the words "With best wishes, Sinclair B. Ferguson", I happened to say to the woman who had asked me to autograph it, "I hope you're not a handwriting analyst". She blushed. "You are!" I responded. "I'd be interested to know what you make of this…" She protested initially, but eventually I persuaded her to analyse my handwriting and tell me what she saw. I was amazed at how much she could accurately tell about my personality from the way I had written half a dozen words. She saw things I had never noticed but which were obvious when she pointed them out to me. (But it would be wise to draw a veil over that!) My personality—what I was—emerged even in scribbling a few words in a book.

It dawned on me then why (back in those days) so many job adverts contained the words "Applicants should apply *in their own handwriting*". I thought the employer simply wanted to know that the applicants could write legibly. But many companies would send the applications to handwriting analysts, asking, "What can you tell us about this individual?"

You don't see job adverts like that today, for a very simple reason. Companies don't need handwriting analysts any longer. Instead, they can examine Twitter accounts and social-media postings. They look for patterns. And these patterns are an index of what we rejoice in—and therefore of who and what we really are.

The chairman of a search committee in a church I served once brought me 3000 tweets posted by a person who seemed to be a strong candidate for a ministry position. The chairman had noticed a disconcerting pattern of what this candidate most rejoiced in. I felt sure the person almost certainly didn't realise it. But it was permanently embedded in a Twitter account for discerning eyes to see.

Do you see the point here? Who we really are emerges in the trivial and incidental details of our lives—in our handwriting, our tweets, and in a thousand other ways. And what we love, what we rejoice in, leaves a permanent mark on our characters; we can never ultimately hide it. Followers of the Truth rejoice in the truth, and that never remains hidden.

So, what do you most rejoice in? In the truth, or in the fact that you won the argument? In the signs of God's generosity to you in a work situation, or in the thought of your own reputation being advanced? In the growth in character you see in your children, or in the relief that they didn't embarrass you in public?

Do you *not* rejoice at wrongdoing? More pointedly, do you not rejoice at wrongdoing even when it happens to someone who has a job you would like, enjoys the admiration you covet, or—for that matter—was guilty of wrongdoing to you?

And if we are people who rejoice with the truth, then it will be the truth of the Christmas message that is our greatest joy at this time of year, even when there are so many other trimmings to enjoy too.

This is the central truth that is worth rejoicing in this Christmas: "The reason the Son of God appeared was to destroy the works of the devil" (1 John 3 v 8). Despite the opposition of the prince of wrongdoing, Christ successfully undid all the wrongdoing that began with Adam (Romans 5 v 12-21). The devil is "a liar and the father of lies" (John 8 v 44), yet "grace and truth came through Jesus Christ" (1 v 17).

The message of Christmas is that Jesus came to a human race that had "exchanged the truth about God for a lie" (Romans 1 v 25). What lie? Genesis 3 explains: the lie about God's word and character—the lie that he is not wholly good and kind, and that his word is not to be trusted. In Jesus, God has exposed that lie for what it is. He gave his Son for us. He thus "shows his love for us" (Romans 5 v 8). In his coming not only did the righteous die for the unrighteous, but the Truth conquered the lie. When we see this, we understand why it is that "love … rejoices with the truth". It isn't simply a matter of wanting to tell the truth. It is that we have come to know the truth, and it has set us free (John 8 v 32). We love the truth, and we become like what we love. Better, we become like the One we love!

The One who was cradled in the manger is the Truth. He said so himself (14 v 6). John saw it: "Grace and truth came through Jesus Christ" (1 v 17). And when we rejoice with the Truth, then we begin to rejoice in everything that is true. Only then are we set free from loving and rejoicing in wrongdoing.

REFLECTION

"Who we really are emerges in the trivial and incidental details of our lives." What are some of the details that reveal your character and what you truly rejoice in?

PRAYER

When first to make my heart his own,
The Lord revealed his mighty grace;
Self reigned, like Dagon, on the throne,
But could not long maintain its place.

It fell, and owned the pow'r divine,
(Grace can with ease the vict'ry gain)
But soon this wretched heart of mine,
Contrived to set it up again.

Again the LORD *his name proclaimed,*
And brought the hateful idol low;
Then self, like Dagon, broken, maimed,
Seemed to receive a mortal blow.

Yet self is not of life bereft,
Nor ceases to oppose his will;
Though but a maimed stump be left,
'Tis Dagon, 'tis an idol still.

Lord! must I always guilty prove,
And idols in my heart have room?
Oh! let the fire of heavenly love,
The very stump of self consume.

John Newton (1725-1807)

14. A COVERING

Love bears all things.

1 Corinthians 13 v 7

I find words interesting. Their sounds are interesting. Their effects are interesting. Their language families are interesting (Latin, Greek, Anglo-Saxon?). And the story of how they came to mean what they do is often fascinating. That's true of the verb Paul uses here: love *bears* all things.

The picture language behind the Greek word for "bears" (*stegō*) may come as a surprise. The verb means "to cover", "to pass over in silence" or "to keep confidential". But in its noun form it means a roof! What's the connection? Simple: a roof covers over the house. It keeps the rain out and protects the household. So, love is like a roof: it prevents leaks; it copes with all weathers; it covers things up—including "a multitude of sins" (1 Peter 4 v 8).

Paul had used the same verb earlier about his ministry to and care for the Corinthians. When he first came to their city, he had taken on a job in a family tent-making business to support himself, rather than accept financial support from them (Acts 18 v 1-3). He had a simple reason for this: "we have not made use of this right [for financial support], but we *endure* anything [the same verb, *stegō*] rather than put an obstacle in the way of the gospel of Christ" (1 Corinthians 9 v 12).

I have a friend who, with his wife, began a ministry to down-and-outs, drug addicts, prostitutes, prisoners, and their families. One day his wife told me something about him that illustrates Paul's point: "You know, he can stand right next to somebody who is stinking, and you wouldn't know whether he noticed the smell or not". We might paraphrase Paul's words to fit my friend, "Love … manages to put up with a stench".

The reason this friend is able to put up with a smell is evident when you meet him. He knows how long Christ put up with him, and now he wants to be like his Saviour. Christ's love for him has created in him a love for others. And that love notices people's needs more than their smells; indeed, in my friend's case, love seems to be more or less leak-proof when it comes to how people smell.

Of course, smells are not the only thing that can get up your nose (excuse the pun!). That is simply an illustration of Paul's general principle: when we love people, we put up with a great deal, just because we love them. We do not love them *because* of their failings any more than Christ loves us "just the way we are", as people sometimes say. It is nearer the truth to say that he loves us despite the way we are. Or to put it another way round: despite the way I am, despite everything about me that offends him, he still loves me.

That is what enabled Paul to devote himself to Christians who were difficult to get on with, as well as those who gave him constant encouragement. The Corinthians certainly fitted into the former category. That was why eventually, although it embarrassed him, he felt he had to speak frankly to them and appeal to them, by describing what he had been willing to bear for the sake of the gospel (2 Corinthians 11 v 16-33).

What explains this? Paul would give the Corinthians the answer to that question too: "The love of Christ controls us" (5 v 14). He didn't mean that he had become a kind of Christian robot, but that Christ's love for him had so gripped him that he could draw only one conclusion. If Christ loved him despite how he was, how could he refuse to love others in the same way? It didn't feel like a big choice to him, and certainly not a special virtue. For Paul, this was just a natural consequence of realising that Jesus loved him, and that he loved him in return.

Paul's love bore all things because Jesus' love first bore all things—including Paul himself.

And Jesus bears you, too.

Because he loved you, he chose to bear the cross and its shame in your place. Now you do not need to bear the judgment of God against your sin—he bore that for you too, in his own body on the tree (1 Peter 2 v 24).

Why? To use the picture language of Paul's vocabulary here, the answer is: to put a roof over our heads—to give us a covering to protect us from the judgment of God on our sins, so that in Christ we might have a hiding place.

You may be familiar with Yom Kippur, the Jewish Day of Atonement. The Hebrew word for "atonement" means "covering". It refers to the mercy seat that covered the ark of the covenant kept in the Most Holy Place in the Jerusalem Temple. That room could be entered only once a year—on the Day of Atonement— and by only one person—the high priest. He went in to the Most Holy Place to sprinkle sacrificial blood on the mercy seat to atone for the people's sins.

It was the most tension-filled moment of the year. The robe he wore beneath his ephod had little bells on it (Exodus 28 v 33-35), apparently so that those outside could hear him moving and be reassured that he had not been struck down dead. It seems that at one time in Israel's history a rope was also tied round his ankle in case he died, so that his body could be pulled out without others having to risk their lives.

The high priest's ministry was a picture of what Jesus came to do. He was anointed as a priest at the age of thirty (Luke 3 v 21-23; Hebrews 5 v 5). He became the mercy seat on which his own sacrificial blood was sprinkled: God "put forward" Jesus "as a propitiation by his blood, to be received by faith" (Romans 3 v 25). He bore our sin. He became a hiding place for us, a roof over our heads.

In the nave of Westminster Abbey in London is a monument to John André, whose remains are buried nearby. It was erected at the expense of King George III. André served as Adjutant General of the British forces during the American Revolutionary War. He was arrested, tried, found guilty of being a British spy, and executed on 2 October 1780. He was so impressive a man that the event caused widespread sadness. When André's body was cut down, a piece of paper was found in his pocket on which he had written out a hymn. It began like this:

Hail, sovereign love, which first began
The scheme to rescue fallen man!
Hail, matchless, free, eternal grace,
That gave my soul a Hiding Place!

We all need that hiding place. The baby in the manger would one day provide it. That is why *Love came down at Christmas*.

REFLECTION

What is God calling you to put up with at present? What difference does it make to know that Jesus bears your sin?

PRAYER

O God, who makes us glad with the yearly remembrance
of the birth of your only Son Jesus Christ,
grant that as we joyfully receive him for our Redeemer,
so we may with sure confidence behold him when he
comes to be our Judge;
who lives and reigns with you and the Holy Spirit,
ever one God, world without end.

> *Gelasian Sacramentary (5th century)*

15. BELIEVING EVERYTHING AND ANYTHING?

Love … believes all things.

1 Corinthians 13 v 7

For most families, the dinner table is at the heart of Christmas Day. Indeed, for many it is at the heart of family life all year round and is often the scene of amusing interchanges.

Our boys had friends round one day, and as they were discussing some aspect of the Christian faith, one of my sons asked, "What do you believe about this, Dad?" I wanted to impress on them that they shouldn't just take my word, but think things through for themselves. So I began my reply, "Well, it doesn't really matter what *I believe…*"

Unfortunately, I paused too long before finishing the sentence. It was the wrong place to pause! One of the boys immediately chided me (I taught in a theological seminary at the time): "Dad! It doesn't matter what you believe?!"

Could I have defended myself by saying, "Well, Paul says, 'Love believes all things'"? Unfortunately, some people have read him that way: *The important thing is having faith—no matter what your religion.* Paul could not possibly have meant that. His letters frequently emphasise the importance of what we believe. Biblical faith has content. Just think how short his letters would have been if he had missed out all the doctrine!

So, we are probably left with one of two ways to understand what Paul means here—each has found support among scholars. Both are consistent with other biblical teaching.

Perhaps Paul meant something like, "Love always seeks to believe the best about people". Love has no natural appetite either to hear (or to tell others) the worst about people. It isn't that love lacks discernment. After all, Jesus told us not to throw pearls to pigs (Matthew 7 v 6). But a loving disposition generously assumes the best of people, instead of leaping to negative conclusions about their actions or motives.

An alternative way of understanding Paul's words is reflected in J.B. Phillips' translation: "Love knows … no end to its trust"; the New International Version goes with "Love … always trusts". Love keeps on trusting, keeps on believing.

Love does, doesn't it? If you love the Lord, you trust him. But why? How do you know he can be trusted absolutely? Because he has proved himself to be entirely trustworthy—the One who will never fail you or let you down. That was why, when David experienced the faithfulness of God to his promises and was delivered from his enemies, he said, "I love you, O Lord…" (Psalm 18 v 1).

David's psalms not only recorded his own experience. They also provided the words by which Jesus most naturally expressed his inner life. That was especially true during his crucifixion. Since our Lord died with words from the psalms on his lips, is it too much of a stretch to think that these words from Psalm 18 were among his first words of praise on Easter Sunday morning? Like a strong man waking from sleep, he rose up from the cold slab in the garden tomb where Nicodemus and Joseph of Arimathea had laid his body on the previous Friday evening. What was he thinking? Read Psalm 18 slowly—and ask (as you should ask about any psalm), "How and when might these words have been on Jesus' mind?" When was he able to look back on an experience of excruciating darkness and express his unfailing love for the God who had shown unfailing love and faithfulness to him?

> *I love you, O Lord, my strength.*
> *The Lord is my rock and my fortress*
> *and my deliverer,*
> *my God, my rock, in whom I take refuge,*
> *my shield, and the horn of my salvation,*
> *my stronghold.*
> *I call upon the Lord, who is worthy to be praised,*
> *and I am saved from my enemies.*
> *The cords of death encompassed me;*

the torrents of destruction assailed me;
the cords of Sheol entangled me;
the snares of death confronted me.
In my distress I called upon the LORD*;*
to my God I cried for help.
From his temple he heard my voice,
and my cry to him reached his ears …

He sent from on high, he took me;
he drew me out of many waters.
He rescued me from my strong enemy
and from those who hated me,
for they were too mighty for me.
They confronted me in the day of my calamity,
but the LORD *was my support.*
He brought me out into a broad place;
he rescued me, because he delighted in me …

Yes, you exalted me above those who rose against me;
you rescued me from the man of violence.

For this I will praise you, O LORD*, among the nations,*
and sing to your name.
Great salvation he brings to his king,
and shows steadfast love to his anointed,
to David and his offspring for ever.
                    (Psalm 18 v 1-6, 16-19, 48-50)

Jesus' cry of dereliction and desolation from the cross, "My God, my God, why have you forsaken me?" comes from the Psalms (Matthew 27 v 46; Psalm 22 v 1). So do the words in which he entrusted himself to God: "Father, into your hands I commit my spirit!" (Luke 23 v 46; Psalm 31 v 5). His love for his Father never failed. And Psalm 18, when placed on the lips of Jesus, essentially says, *Father, I kept my promises to you; and you have kept all your promises to me—and to all who will come to trust in me.*

The cross and the empty tomb tell us something. They prove that all of God's promises can be trusted. For the promise that his Son would suffer in our place (Isaiah 53 v 4-6) was surely the hardest promise the Father ever made. And he kept it. In fact, says Paul, "all the promises of God find their Yes in him [Christ]" (2 Corinthians 1 v 20).

What does God promise to you this Christmas and beyond? He promises to forgive all your sins when you turn from them. He promises always to hear you when you call to him. He promises only to work for your good. He promises to walk alongside you through all the hard times, and bring you safely into his presence in heaven. If you love him, you will trust him. How? By remembering that God has already kept his hardest-to-keep promise in Christ—from his makeshift cradle to his empty grave.

REFLECTION

In what ways has God proved himself to be entirely trustworthy to you? Which of his promises do you most need to hold onto today?

PRAYER

> *O God, from whom to be turned is to fall,*
> *to whom to be turned is to rise,*
> *and with whom to stand*
> *is to abide forever;*
> *grant us in all our duties your help,*
> *in all our perplexities your guidance,*
> *in all our dangers your protection,*
> *and in all our sorrows your peace,*
> *through Jesus Christ our Lord.*
>
> *Augustine of Hippo (354-430)*

16. HOPE SPRINGS ETERNAL

Love ... hopes all things.

1 Corinthians 13 v 7

When we say, "I hope so" we do not usually mean the same thing as the New Testament does. We may be hoping for a white Christmas, even although the weatherman is predicting "sunny and cold with occasional showers". That is not hope but wishful thinking.

What then is hope? Imagine a child catching a glimpse of his father sneaking something into the house—something that is difficult to carry and has two big wheels. If later you were to ask him, "What are you hoping for this Christmas", he would reply with a big grin, "I am hoping for a new bicycle!" "Do you think you'll get it?" "Oh yes, I am sure!" That is hope in the biblical sense. It is being sure that you will receive something you don't yet have.

So, when Paul says, "Love ... hopes all things", he is not just describing a glass-half-full kind of person who always "hopes for the best". He means somebody who believes the promises of God and is waiting for them to be fulfilled—no matter what.

The Christian is, by definition, a hopeful person. That hope is not artificial self-projection. It is produced in us by God's promises. Because we love and trust the Lord, we believe the promises he has given in his word. They have become the spectacle lenses through which we view everything—and that is what injects the melody of hope into our lives.

But what does Paul mean by saying, "Love … hopes all things"? He means that we have an underlying confidence that God will be with us and bless us just as he has promised, even when life is at its worst.

But surely such confident assurance does not belong to the real world? Our lives are full of disappointed hopes—in relationships, at work, in a thousand experiences in life. Is Paul advocating an ostrich-like, head-in-the-sand way to live?

No—Paul knew plenty of pain and disappointment. One look at his back would have assured you of that. Later, in words that filled him with embarrassment, he described what you would see there: evidence of "countless beatings". "Five times I received from the Jews the forty lashes less one. Three times I was beaten with rods. Once I was stoned. Three times I was shipwrecked; a night and a day I was adrift at sea…" (2 Corinthians 11 v 23-25).

This doesn't sound like a naïve hope-for-the-best kind of man! Paul was a realist, especially about the tough times he faced as a Christian. Yet he makes the striking claim that "hope does not put us to shame"; it doesn't let us down or disappoint us. Why? Because "God's love has been poured into our hearts through the Holy Spirit who has been given to us" (Romans 5 v 5).

What does this mean? Our biggest hope is for everlasting life: for heaven and all that will follow it in the new heavens and earth. Being sure of that, even although we don't yet experience it, changes everything. It is like light appearing at the end of the tunnel, dispersing the total darkness that engulfs us. It enables us to see our way forward.

Paul's point is this: heaven is a world of love. From that heaven God sends the Spirit of his Son into our hearts. He brings heaven's love down to earth and floods our hearts with a sense of it. We know we are loved. We are sure of our place in heaven because God the Father has given us his promise. But we are also sure of it because the Holy Spirit has brought the atmosphere and love of heaven down to us here and now!

Love incarnate—Jesus Christ—came down to earth at Christmas. He did so to stoop further down—to the humiliating death on the cross for our sin and its shame (yes, he died for our shame too). But he stooped to conquer. He rose again in triumph over sin, death, and Satan. Since he did all this for us, his resurrection is the guarantee of the resurrection of all who belong to him.

Paul had an impressive way of putting this to the Corinthians. They were accusing him of vacillating—was he coming to visit them or wasn't he? He replied that he was a follower of Christ. His yes meant yes, just like Jesus! For "all the promises of God find their Yes in him" (2 Corinthians 1 v 15-24).

The incarnation, the birth of the Christ-child is, as we have seen, the ultimate "Yes" to the promises of God. But why?

First, because it means God has kept his *oldest promise*, recorded in Genesis 3 v 15. There would be ongoing conflict—between the seed (or descendants) of the serpent and the seed of the woman; and then, ultimately, between one Seed of the woman and the serpent himself. The older artists who pictured the infant Jesus with a serpent being crushed underneath his foot understood this well. God has kept that promise. When we sing the first verse of "O Little Town of Bethlehem" we are reminded of this:

> *O little town of Bethlehem,*
> *How still we see thee lie!*
> *Above thy deep and dreamless sleep*
> *The silent stars go by.*
> *Yet in thy dark streets shineth*
> *The everlasting Light;*
> *The hopes and fears of all the years*
> *Are met in thee tonight.*
>
> *Phillips Brooks (1835-1893)*

"The hopes ... of all the years" converged there on the first Christmas Eve. And if God has kept this, his oldest promise, can we not also be sure that he will keep all his promises? That is the hope of love.

But the incarnation not only means the longest-standing promise of God has been fulfilled. Second, it means that the *costliest promise* of God has been fulfilled. God keeping his promise meant his Son would suffer and die. To keep his promise of forgiveness, freedom and eternal life, he "did not spare his own Son but gave him up for us all" (Romans 8 v 32). Paul draws the logical conclusion: since this is the case, we can be sure God will withhold nothing from us that is for our ultimate good.

The logic goes like this: if you spend £500 to pay for a holiday, but then discover there is an additional £10 taxi fare to be paid to get you from the airport to your destination, you're not going to turn back. No, since you have already paid so much, of course you will pay the extra. The same logic applies here. If God has kept his major promise by giving his Son for you and to you, you can be sure he will keep every promise he has made.

That is why his love is the foundation not only for faith but also for hope. And that hope lasts; it will never fail. It is a hope that we can hold on to even when we are suffering, even when life seems to be unravelling at the seams, even when our worst nightmares are coming true. We can still have hope, because God kept his biggest promise, his oldest and costliest promise, when *Love came down at Christmas*.

REFLECTION

What difference will the certain hope of heaven—"a world of love"—make to how you live and who you love this week?

PRAYER

Merciful Lord,
the comforter and teacher of your faithful people,
increase in your church the desires
which you have given,
and confirm the hearts of those who hope in you
by enabling them to understand
the depth of your promises,
that all your adopted children may even now behold,
with the eyes of faith,
and patiently wait for,
the light which as yet you do not openly manifest,
through Jesus Christ our Lord, Amen.

Ambrose of Milan (337-397)

17. ENDURANCE TEST

Love ... endures all things.

1 Corinthians 13 v 7

The Christian life is an endurance test. I remember reading as a teenager Paul's famous words about the Christian warfare and armour (Ephesians 6 v 10-20). I paused at verses 13-14: "Take up the whole armour of God, that you may be able to withstand in the evil day". Great! But then Paul goes on, "... and having done all, to stand firm. Stand therefore..." I still remember thinking, "Is that it? Is that all? Is that the sum total—just 'standing'? Surely there must be much more. What about 'the victorious Christian life' and 'Life with a capital L'?"

I am showing my age by mentioning these descriptions of the Christian life! But there are contemporary versions. Here, for example, is the description of a recent Christian book: "Just like Superman, who can leap over any hurdle to defeat every foe, followers of Christ have the supernatural ability to conquer the challenges we face". In comparison, Paul's words about simply managing to remain standing don't seem too impressive. Looking back on my own Christian life, far from having been like Superman, it seems almost miraculous that I am still standing!

In 1 Corinthians 13, Paul is like an expert jeweller examining the famous "Love Diamond". You can almost imagine him with his little loupe in his eye, slowly turning "Love" round to the light, examining every facet. He sees things most of us don't notice and points out features we would probably ignore. He does that here. Love *endures all things*.

He had already said that love "is patient" and that it "bears all things". What he says now sounds very similar: love "endures all things". But there is a difference. He uses three different words. Here "endures" is the verb "to remain" or "stay" with a prefix which implies the idea of being "underneath" or "below". Endurance is the ability to "remain underneath".

Picture the weight-lifting competitions at the Olympic Games. Rubbing white chalk onto his hands, his belt in position, his upper body bulging with strength, the competitor steps onto the dais, puts his hands on the barbells, takes deep breaths, snatches them up in one movement, and then jerks them above his head in another. He is lifting over 250 kilos, or 500 pounds (that's like lifting three men above your head!). His arms tremble, his body shudders under the weight. But he manages to remain stable. He's still standing. He's given the green light. Down go the barbells, bouncing on the floor, and he raises his arms in a gesture of satisfied triumph.

You would need to be a cynic to say, "All he did was to remain standing. Anyone could do that!" No, he remained standing under tremendous pressure. That is what Paul says love does.

Remember Asaph, the often-struggling director of music in the Jerusalem Temple? When he wandered around the city, he saw people who despised his faith (and probably his psalms as well!). He thought, "Their bodies are fat and sleek. They are not in trouble as others are ... pride is their necklace" (Psalm 73 v 4-6). He was honest enough to say, "I was envious of the arrogant when I saw the prosperity of the wicked" (v 3). But then he went back up the hill to the temple. There he saw things as they really are (v 17). He had been looking through the wrong end of the telescope. He says, "My feet had almost stumbled, my steps had nearly slipped" (v 2). But now, in the temple, he is on his feet again. He is still standing. He is able to "endure" the pressures. In the temple he rediscovers God's covenant love expressed in Scripture and song and sacrifice. The knowledge of that love keeps his love going.

Psalms 73 – 83 are all psalms of Asaph. Every one of them describes his struggles. He is like a weight-lifter coming onto the dais, uncertain whether he can "remain under" the weight of the pressures he feels. But at the end he is still standing and able to say: "You alone, whose name is the LORD, are the Most High over all the earth" (Psalm 83 v 18). Do you notice the way the word "LORD" is written? In modern translations

"Lord" (rather than "Lord") represents the Hebrew word *Yahweh*, the great covenant name for God, the name he revealed to Moses (Exodus 3 v 13-14; 6 v 2-8). It's God's personal name, which he gives to his people to use—it reminds them that he is their faithful God, the One who is committed to them in love. So, you can see what it was that turned Asaph's perspective around: the knowledge of the love of the loving God, Yahweh, the Lord. It is that which will keep us standing. It is his love which holds us fast.

When Jesus was born in Bethlehem, there was no room for him in the inn. The Son of God was lowered from heaven into a wooden feeding trough for a cradle. But in a sense, this was prophetic of his whole life—as a roaming preacher, he had nowhere to lay his head (Matthew 8 v 20). But it was true especially of his death. At the end of his life he was cradled once more by wood when he was lifted up to be crucified.

It was then that darkness descended, not only on the land, but also over Jesus. Then came the only time in his life when he felt that the Lord of love had abandoned him. His experience was darker than Asaph's. He no longer felt "you hold my right hand" (as Asaph did in Psalm 73 v 23). Instead the words of Psalm 22 v 1 expressed his sense of dereliction: "My God, my God, why have you forsaken me?" He came under the crushing weight of God's wrath against us, and it left him without any sense of his love. He felt there was no room for him on earth or in heaven. But his love endured all things. Rather than call on twelve legions of angels to deliver him, his arms remained outstretched like the cosmic weightlifter he was, bearing the sins of the world. In his love for his Father and for us he remained obedient, still trusting, even in his desolation, and continuing to call God "*my* God". At that moment his love for his Father was tested to the limit, and it endured.

How could this be? It was because Jesus knew in advance that in Calvary's darkness, when he felt abandoned, that would actually be the time when his Father's love for him would know no bounds. Earlier he had told his disciples, "For this reason the Father loves me, because I lay down my life" (John 10 v 17). Can we imagine the Father singing, as Christians have often done?

> *My Jesus, I love thee, I know thou art mine ...*
> *If ever I loved thee, my Jesus 'tis now.*

The Son of God knew God's plan for our salvation before he ever undertook his mission. He entered the darkness of Mary's womb knowing full well that it would lead to the deeper darkness of the agony of Gethsemane and Calvary. But because "Love ... endures all", he kept going.

So what is it that you feel the weight of today? What circumstances seem to be bearing down on you? In what relationship do you feel at the end of your tether? Take heart—your love can endure all things, because Christ has endured all things for you. His love will keep you standing.

REFLECTION

Why was Christ's love able to endure the cross? How does that moment in history enable your love to endure today?

PRAYER

Love divine, all loves excelling,
Joy of heaven to earth come down;
Fix in us thy humble dwelling;
All thy faithful mercies crown!
Jesus, thou art all compassion,
Pure unbounded love thou art;
Visit us with thy salvation;
Enter every trembling heart.

Finish, then, thy new creation;
Pure and spotless let us be.
Let us see thy great salvation
Perfectly restored in thee;
Changed from glory into glory,
Till in heaven we take our place,
Till we cast our crowns before thee,
Lost in wonder, love, and praise.

Charles Wesley (1707-1788)

18. EVERLASTING LOVE

Love never ends. As for prophecies, they will pass away; as for tongues, they will cease; as for knowledge, it will pass away.

1 Corinthians 13 v 8

What are the *really important* things in your church, and in your own Christian life?

In Corinth they seem to have been being able to prophesy, speaking in tongues, and having special knowledge. Paul did not have a bad word to say about any of these gifts in themselves (although he did issue guidelines for using them). The spiritual gifts Christ gives to his church are never the problem. But the recipients sometimes are.

Paul has already told us that it is possible to speak with the tongues of men and angels, have all knowledge, and the gift of prophecy, and mountain-moving faith—but amount to nothing. How so? Because you are "nothing" if you think that the really important thing about you is your gifts.

A man in a congregation I once served sometimes phoned me on Mondays to encourage me to stick to writing books (in case his point doesn't register, he had been listening to me preach the day before!). I managed to maintain some sense of proportion because he also tended to complain that he had never been made an elder in the church. Then during one conversation he told me he was worth both myself and my predecessor added together.

Two thoughts crossed my mind (at least two that I am willing to share!). The first was that if you *subtracted* whatever gifts I had from my predecessor's, he would still be more gifted than my less-than-encouraging caller. The second was that even if my caller had the gifts he claimed, he did not seem to understand that the ability to complain is not a qualification for leadership in the church!

That (I hope!) is a fairly extreme example. But it illustrates Paul's point. Gifts are secondary; love is primary. Gifts are tools. What matters is how a person employs them.

Now Paul takes a step further to emphasise his point. One day all these gifts—speaking in tongues, prophesying, having special knowledge—will come to an end. Love, in contrast, won't.

Paul seems to have had an interest in words. He realised the gospel is so unique that sometimes it needs its own vocabulary—he may even have created words to serve that purpose. And he used words that probably conjured up pictures in the minds of his readers.

This statement may be a case in point. When he says that love doesn't end, he uses a verb that means to slip or to fall. Love does not slip and fall. It is steady and reliable. It endures. Some scholars have thought that he used this verb because he remembered the road between Athens and Corinth (Acts 18 v 1 records him making that trip). Part of that road was dangerous. Strabo, the well-known geographer of antiquity, wrote this about it: "The road approaches so close to the rocks that in many places it goes along the edge of precipices, because the mountain that lies above them is high and it would be impractical to build a road there." Perhaps, as Paul made that journey, he wondered how many people had stumbled, fallen, and gone over the edge.

Love never falls or fails. But one day all of these spiritual gifts—no matter how important they seemed to the Corinthians—would come to an end. They would no longer be needed. But love will never be redundant. It will never pass away or cease.

Does this all sound more romantic than realistic? Perhaps you know too much of broken hearts or cold relationships to believe that "love never ends".

But remember, Paul wants to fix our eyes on Christ's love—a love that didn't float in romance and rose-petals, but was grounded in reality. We're reminded of that in the upper room, the night before Jesus died.

You know what it is like when you are facing a difficult experience. The time has been set. The nearer it gets the more it seems to dominate your mind. It seems to separate you from everyone else. It produces a kind of focus, a concentration, a tension. Everything else seems incidental. Other people and their problems fade into the background.

But what if that difficult experience were your crucifixion? More, what if you knew that you would be utterly alone, suffering agonising pain and asphyxiation, but in addition you would feel that the God who is Love had himself forsaken you? What would you do the day before?

What did Love do?

John's Gospel is in two sections (chapters 1 – 12 and chapters 13 – 21). Each section begins with a kind of prologue. Both describe the love or grace of Jesus.

The first prologue does it in high theological terms:

In the beginning was the Word,
and the Word was with God [face to face with God],
and the Word was God ...
And the Word became flesh and dwelt among us,
and we have seen his glory [so he came face to face
with us].   *(John 1 v 1, 14)*

But the second section (chapters 13 – 21) also has a prologue. It conveys the same message but in the context of a small upper room somewhere in Jerusalem the day before Jesus' crucifixion:

Jesus, knowing ... that he had come from God
and was going back to God ...
laid aside his outer garments, and taking a towel ...
began to wash the disciples' feet.   *(John 13 v 3-5)*

John explains why Jesus did this: "Having loved his own who were in the world, he loved them to the end" (13 v 1). Jesus was enacting the story of his incarnation—his coming from his place of honour at the table of heaven to kneel in a world of dirty feet for his disciples. He was stooping down for them. Faced with their sin, and with his impending sacrifice for it on the cross, his love lasted "to the end" (v 1). He was ready to do whatever it took, whatever it cost. The foot-washing was a dramatic picture of how much he loved his disciples. His love never fails. It never falls. It never ends. It lasts.

This is the love that is poured out into Christians' hearts by the Holy Spirit (Romans 5 v 5). It is why we love. And it is what reassures and empowers us in those moments when we feel our love is failing—we can cry out to the Spirit to fill us with a love that never ends. He is sure to help us, because Christ's unfailing *love came down at Christmas.*

REFLECTION

In what circumstances are you currently relying on God's love to "never fail"? How does the fact that Christ's love endured the cross give you hope?

PRAYER

You who are the light of the minds that know you,
the life of the souls that love you,
and the strength of the thoughts that seek you;
help us to know you
that we may truly love you,
so to love you
that we may fully serve you,
whose service is perfect freedom,
through Jesus Christ our Lord. Amen.

Augustine (354-430)

19. FUTURE PERFECT

For we know in part and we prophesy in part,
but when the perfect comes, the partial will pass away.

1 Corinthians 13 v 9

S ome Christians (and whole churches) have a tendency to emphasise their "distinctives".

Some are "committed to expository preaching",
while others are "seeker-sensitive" or "missional"—or
whatever. In your church the "distinctive" may be "dis-
cipleship" or "small groups" or the evangelistic "pro-
gramme" you use; or that your church belongs to one or
other group within your denomination or beyond it. Or
it may be that what defines your church is your denomination. Or even that you belong to no denomination.

The church in Corinth also had distinctives. It is the
only New Testament church which we know for sure
had services where there was speaking in tongues as
well as prophecy. Apparently they were "not lacking in
any spiritual gift" (1 Corinthians 1 v 7).

But in addition to having gifts, the Corinthians had
a major problem. They were defining themselves in
terms of their gifts, not realising that these were partial

and temporary, not complete and final. Paul says this very pointedly: *Don't you see that your knowledge is partial and that in its very nature prophecy is given and understood only piece by piece? The complete, the perfect, is still to come.* He had already implied this in his previous statement: tongues will cease, special "knowledge" will pass away, prophecy will be no more. The same could be said of some of the "gifts" that feature prominently in churches today. For example, one day the role of "worship-leaders" will be no more. In heaven Jesus is the worship-leader (in fact, he already is on earth according to Hebrews 2 v 12!).

Knowing *when* this would take place—the question Christians today often debate—would not have solved the Corinthians' problem. It might well have exacerbated it—would they then have become the one church that knew when these gifts would cease to function? The real problem was not lack of knowledge. It was a lack of humility and a lack of love. The fact that they focused on the partial and not on the permanent made that clear.

It is easy to be blinded by gifts, especially unusual, inexplicable or spectacular ones. We have the same tendency as the Corinthians—we look at them through the wrong end of the telescope. People who have them seem big; others (including ourselves) seem small by comparison.

"When the perfect comes", the extraordinary insights of the gifts of knowledge and prophecy and the ability to speak in other tongues will be seen for what they are—only partial, only little pieces. In fact, it takes all the gifts Christ has given to our church family to put him on display—and even then, we do that only partially. The day has not yet arrived when we will see him "face to face" (1 Corinthians 13 v 12)—all in one piece as it were. Understanding this breeds humility because it underlines the "not-yet-ness" of our present Christian experience.

Like the Corinthians, we have been given gifts to enable us to kneel before each other in love and say, "I have something here that Jesus has given me to pass on to you. He loves you. He has given this gift to me so that I can have a way of expressing my love for you too. Please receive it from me, because it is 'for the common good' (12 v 7) and for 'building up the church' (14 v 12)". But our gifts are only partial. Only a fragment of who Jesus is and how much he loves us is expressed in our gifts.

In the world to come it would not be necessary for the Corinthians to have the gifts of tongues or words of knowledge, or to prophesy, in order to show Christ's love—for then they would all see him fully and perfectly, "face to face" (13 v 12; 1 John 3 v 2). Knowing this should have taught them that what really matters is knowing Christ better and showing his love more consistently. All spiritual gifts are merely temporary means to that end.

Paul told the Corinthians he could not really speak to them as mature adults. They were "as infants in Christ" (1 Corinthians 3 v 1). They enjoyed others admiring them and so they used their gifts to say something about themselves rather than about Christ. There was all too little of the spirit of the upper room foot-washing (John 13 v 1-20), and too much of the upper room position-seeking (Luke 22 v 24-27). And, sadly, this was true even although the Corinthians had seen the way Paul had used his gifts. He spoke in tongues more than all of them (1 Corinthians 14 v 18)! But he did not preach himself but "Jesus Christ as Lord". And that carried an implication: "[We are] your servants [*douloi*, bond-slaves] for Jesus' sake" (2 Corinthians 4 v 5). After all, *charismata* (grace gifts) are intended to express the grace of the Lord Jesus Christ, who impoverished himself to make others rich (8 v 9).

How sad if we can celebrate Christmas but miss this!

Elsewhere Paul prays that Christians will come to "comprehend with all the saints what is the breadth and length and height and depth, and to know the love of Christ that surpasses knowledge" (Ephesians 3 v 18-19).

How do we measure such love?

- We measure love by the greatness of the person who loves.
- We measure love by the gulf between the one who loves and the one who is loved.
- We measure love by what it is willing to do for the loved one.
- We measure love by how long it lasts.

By these measurements the special gifts we have are but very small expressions of the perfect. At the end of the day, when they stood before Christ, the Corinthians were not likely to be asked, "So, what was your gift? Special knowledge others lacked? Tongues others could not speak? Prophecies about things others did not know?" No—far more important would be their answer to Christ's question, "What posture did you adopt towards your fellow Christians—did you kneel before them then, as you kneel before me now? For 'as you did it to one of the least of these my brothers, you did it to me.'" (Philippians 2 v 10; Matthew 25 v 40)

It seems that the measure of how we use our gifts will be in whether we were prepared to use them to love the least of the brothers and sisters.

The Corinthians had been taught the Christmas message. They knew "the grace of our Lord Jesus Christ, that though he was rich, yet for [their] sake he became poor" (2 Corinthians 8 v 9). But they had not appreciated its implications. How different things would have been if they had used their gifts on their knees, saying, "I am your servant for Jesus' sake. Receive his love through my service. And please accept it with my love too."

That is what God is calling you to this Christmas: to get on your knees before others and show them Christ's love. This is rarely easy, or fun, or comfortable—but it is possible, when you understand why *Love came down at Christmas*.

REFLECTION

"Only a fragment of who Jesus is and how much he loves us is expressed in our gifts." In what way does that truth both challenge and encourage you?

PRAYER

Merciful and most loving God,
by whose will and bountiful gift Jesus Christ our Lord
humbled himself that he might exalt humankind;
and became flesh
that he might restore us in the most celestial image;
and was born of the virgin
that he might uplift the lowly;
grant us the inheritance of the meek,
perfect in us your likeness,
and bring us at the last to rejoice
in beholding your beauty,
and with all your saints to glory in your grace;
through the same Jesus Christ our Lord, Amen.
Gallican Sacramentary (8th century)

20. GROWING UP

When I was a child, I spoke like a child, I thought like a child, I reasoned like a child. When I became a man, I gave up childish ways.

1 Corinthians 13 v 11

It seems that no matter what gift you give to toddlers, they are always much more interested in the Christmas wrapping paper than in the present it contains. This phenomenon is usually met with coos of delight and general amusement among the adults. After all, there is something undeniably attractive in infants acting as infants.

But if you see your seven-year-old doing the same thing, you might be a little anxious that he is not developing properly. If you were to see an eighteen-year-old disregarding the games console and climbing inside the cardboard box instead, you'd be concerned that something was seriously wrong.

Paul says that, spiritually speaking, you and I are often like fully grown adults playing in a cardboard box. That was certainly true of the Corinthians.

Helping people grow to full spiritual maturity in Christ lay near the heart of Paul's ministry. He told the Christians in Colossae that he wanted to "present everyone mature in Christ" and added, "For this I toil, struggling with all his energy that he powerfully works within me" (Colossians 1 v 28-29).

Of course new converts do not mature overnight. Paul had spent a full eighteen months with the Corinthians, helping them to grow. But he was not seeing the maturity he desired—rather the reverse. He had already told them that he couldn't treat them like adults because they were behaving like spiritual infants (he uses the same word—child, or infant (*nēpios*)—in 1 Corinthians 3 v 1 and 13 v 11).

Distressingly, instead of putting away "childish ways", they seemed to think these were marks of spiritual maturity. They were like children who begin to smoke cigarettes at the age of nine, thinking they are being grown up, when they are only revealing their immaturity and lack of discernment.

Several things were stunting the Corinthians' growth—and we'd be wise to consider whether they are stunting our growth, too.

We have already seen that the Corinthians had an unhealthy interest in ranking preachers, not realising that they were depriving themselves of the privilege of the ministry of them all. Imagine being in a church where you had the opportunity to hear Simon Peter, Paul the apostle, and Apollos preach! Arguing about which one was best meant that they were denying themselves the blessings God wanted to give them through all three of them.

And then they were lacking in discernment. They were enamoured of certain more spectacular spiritual gifts and had lost sight of the importance of love.

Earlier in his letter, Paul points out other signs of their immaturity. They had not taken nearly seriously enough the fact that there was blatant sin in the church fellowship (chapter 5); they were disgracing the name of Christ by some of their behaviour patterns (chapter 6).

But two other symptoms of their stunted growth were particularly significant.

The first was that, when it came to life choices, their view was that they could do whatever they wanted so long as it was "lawful" or there was "nothing wrong with it" (6 v 12; 10 v 23). Perhaps you recognise that tendency.

But for Paul, that is the response of an immature Christian—if a Christian at all. It misses the point. It fails to ask the most important question: is this for the glory of the Lord? Earlier he had suggested ways in which they could tell whether that was true or not:

- Will this really help advance our Christian life (6 v 12)?
- Will this have a tendency to enslave me (v 12)?
- Will this help me to become a mature believer (10 v 23)?
- Will this be a real help to my fellow Christians (v 24)?

These are the kinds of questions that we ought to ask as we decide where to spend our time, how to use our money, and what our plans are for the year ahead.

The second symptom of the Corinthians' stunted growth was the perspective they had on worship. Their focus was on their personal gifts. That was (and is) a form of narcissism, not a recipe for ministry. They were far too concerned with the spectacular and the unusual in worship, and with what their gifts said about them. Paul was far more concerned about what is central in worship: namely, the presence of God among his people, so that if "an unbeliever or outsider enters, he is convicted by all, he is called to account by all, the secrets of his heart are disclosed, and so, falling on his face, he will worship God and declare that God is really among you" (14 v 24-25).

So Paul could not speak to the Corinthians as grown-up Christians. Like the author of Hebrews, he could have written to them, "You need milk, not solid food" for "solid food is for the mature, for those who have their powers of discernment trained by constant practice to distinguish good from evil" (Hebrews 5 v 12-14). They simply lacked a focus on the glory of God and the presence of wisdom in their thinking, in their assessments, and in their choices.

Alas, the Corinthians had forgotten something about Jesus. As he grew physically, he also grew spiritually. And by the time he was twelve, he had "increased in wisdom ... and in favour with God" (Luke 2 v 52). He kept on growing in discernment and in his Father's favour.

Perhaps—like many Christians—they had given little thought to this. If so, they were thinking of Jesus as an idea rather than as a real person who was fully and truly man. They had not reflected on the fact that the commitment of the Son of God to the incarnation was also a commitment to grow and develop not only physically (beginning as an embryo in the womb and growing into full manhood), but also in experience, and in obedience ("He learned obedience through what he suffered", Hebrews 5 v 8)—and in favour with God.

Jesus' obedience to his Father grew through every test he faced until the final examination, when he became "obedient to the point of death, even death on a cross" (Philippians 2 v 8). As a child, he had loved his parents. As a twelve-year-old boy, he had lovingly obeyed the fifth commandment, although his parents had misunderstood him (Exodus 20 v 12; Luke 2 v 51). He filled to the full the loving obedience of a pre-teenager. His wilderness temptations were a yet greater test that called for greater expressions of that love for his Father. And his crucifixion called for the final fulfilment of that loving obedience which he had shown more and more as it was tested throughout the whole course of his life.

If the Master kept on growing, what does that say about his servants? Do not settle for speaking like a child, thinking like a child and reasoning like a child. It's time to give up being childish, and live for the glory of the Lord.

REFLECTION

In what ways might your Christian growth be "stunted"? How will you ask God to grow you?

PRAYER

O Jesus Christ, grow thou in me,
And all things else recede!
My heart be daily nearer thee,
From sin be daily freed.

More of thy glory let me see,
Thou Holy, Wise and True!
I would thy living image be,
In joy and sorrow, too.

Fill me with gladness from above,
Hold me by strength divine;
Lord, make the glow of thy great love,
Through my whole being shine.

Make this poor self grow less and less,
Be thou my life and aim;
O make me daily through thy grace,
More meet to bear thy Name!

Johann C. Lavater (1741-1841)

21. FACE TO FACE

For now we see in a mirror dimly,
but then face to face.

1 Corinthians 13 v 12

After eighteen months in Corinth, Paul must have been very familiar with daily life there. The city—as we have seen—was famous for its metalwork. That included making metal mirrors.

It has sometimes been suggested that Paul is implying (by the words "now we see in a mirror dimly") that ancient Corinthian mirrors were of poor quality. It seems more likely though that Paul is contrasting two different ways of seeing: "dimly" or indirectly (via a mirror) and clearly or directly (face to face). You see only indirectly in a mirror. You see a person's reflection, not the person himself. Seeing "face to face" is a very different experience.

John tells us that "No one has ever seen God" (John 1 v 18). True, "the LORD used to speak to Moses face to face, as a man speaks to his friend" (Exodus 33 v 11). But we're told later that Moses could *not* in fact see God's face (v 20—no one could see God's face and live). In this sense, Moses was certainly brought into the near presence of God; but the time had not yet come for mankind to see his face.

All that changed with the incarnation. It enabled what Moses could not experience. The new covenant provides what the old lacked, because "the Word became flesh and dwelt among us, and we have seen his glory, glory as of the only Son from the Father, full of grace and truth" (John 1 v 14). The Word was *with God* (that is, he was "face to face" with God, v 1) and "became flesh" *with us*. In the incarnation, the Son of God became visible in order to be face to face with us as well as face to face with his Father. John saw his glory "as of the only Son from the Father" (v 14). Paul also saw "the light of the knowledge of the glory of God in the face of Jesus Christ" (2 Corinthians 4 v 6).

We see him too—in the pages of the Bible. It is the Christian's mirror. When we look into it, we see him reflected. Although we cannot see him directly, we find ourselves "beholding the glory of the Lord" (3 v 18). We "see" him with the eyes of faith and come to know him. But the Bible, the God-breathed word—no matter how wonderful it is, no matter how clear a picture of Jesus it reflects—is not Jesus himself. The Bible was not born for us, nor was it crucified for our sins; nor did it rise and ascend into heaven for our justification and glorification. Only Jesus did that. The Bible does make us wise for salvation through faith in Christ (2 Timothy 3 v 15). It is absolutely reliable. But the reason we love reading its pages is because we see reflected in them the face of our Saviour. We must beware falling in love with our learning instead of our Lord.

One day we will have no need of the Bible. We will no longer need the mirror that is so essential to us here, for we will see him face to face. "We know that when he appears we shall be like him, *because we shall see him as he is*" (1 John 3 v 2).

I am reminded of a very vivid dream I had as a young Christian. In it I had died and gone to heaven! I was surprised to be greeted and welcomed by friends who were already there, although they were just a little older than I was. But as they crowded round to greet me, I saw myself (in the dream) pushing them away and heard myself saying, "Let me get to Jesus! I want to see Jesus!" I have always felt slightly guilty about the fact that I might have been caught pushing in heaven! But the words I heard myself speak have been a constant reminder to me of the heart and goal of the Christian life: "Let me get to Jesus. I want to see Jesus!"

At the Advent season—at least since the 12th century—Christians have reflected on the three-fold coming of the Lord Jesus: his first coming at Bethlehem to dwell among us in humility; his final coming at the end of time to dwell among us in glory; but also his coming again and again, in between these two moments—when he comes to dwell in the hearts of those who trust him as their Saviour and Lord (Ephesians 3 v 17).

Christ's first advent is the guarantee of his final return. But through his coming to dwell in our hearts we experience the wonder of the love he expressed in his incarnation, and the assurance that we will be with him for ever when he returns. So there is something particularly appropriate for believers in Christmas Eve services so often beginning with Cecil Frances Alexander's hymn, "Once in Royal David's City". It gives us an opportunity to sing of both the manger in the cattle shed and of Christ's coming again in glory:

And our eyes at last shall see him,
Through his own redeeming love …

Not in that poor lowly stable,
With the oxen standing by,
We shall see him but in heaven,
Set at God's right hand on high,
And he leads his children on
To the place where he is gone.

Today we see him dimly, in the mirror of God's word. But then we will see him face to face—what a day that will be!

As a young man my late friend R.C. Sproul often helped to bring his sickly father to the dinner table. After his father's death, he had a recurring dream in which he would meet his father again. But his father was unchanged, still sickly and weak. R.C. could not understand. The dream continued to puzzle and to haunt him. Then one night he dreamed that he was in heaven and once again met his father. But now he was well and strong and able to guide him around. After a while R.C.

asked his father, "But Dad, where do we go in order to see the glory?" His father answered, "Son, we don't need to go anywhere. The glory is everywhere."

That much is true—not because R.C. dreamt it but because the Bible says it. In that world there is "no temple in the city, for its temple is the Lord God the Almighty and the Lamb. And the city has no need of sun or moon to shine on it, for the glory of God gives it light, and its lamp is the Lamb." (Revelation 21 v 22-23) Can you imagine seeing the face that illumines all heaven with the brilliance of its glory?

The first advent is meant to make you long for the second advent. Our celebrations of joy this Christmas are only a kind of reverberating echo of the joy we will know in the future when at last we come face to face with Jesus.

REFLECTION

The Bible is a mirror through which we see Jesus—what difference ought that make to the way that you approach God's word? How will your celebrations this Christmas point you to the joy of seeing Jesus at his second coming?

PRAYER

Grant, O God, of your mercy,
that we may come to everlasting life,
and there beholding your glory as it is,
may equally say:

Glory to the Father who created us,
Glory to the Son who redeemed us,
Glory to the Holy Spirit who sanctified us.
Glory to the most high and undivided Trinity,
Whose works are inseparable,
Whose kingdom without end abides,
From age to age, for ever. Amen.

Augustine (354-430)

22. THE PART IS NOT THE WHOLE

Now I know in part; then I shall know fully, even as I have been fully known.

1 Corinthians 13 v 12

Have you ever spent a lot of money and a considerable amount of time preparing the perfect Christmas gift for someone… only for them to brush it aside? Sometimes our best efforts at expressing our love are rebuffed.

In the upper room, Simon Peter proved to be very resistant to the way Jesus expressed the fact that "having loved his own who were in the world, he loved them to the end" (John 13 v 1). How could his Master rise from supper, take off his outer garments, wind the slave's towel round his waist, pour water into a basin, and then, kneeling before each of his disciples, wash their dirty feet?

What a display of love! But it was not to Simon Peter's taste and he protested. Jesus' response is significant: "What I am doing you do not understand now, but afterwards you will understand" (v 7). He was referring to the foot-washing. But his words also applied more broadly to Peter's whole experience with Jesus. The Master knew what he was doing; Peter would only understand "afterwards".

Jesus could have said the same to Abraham, or to Jacob, or to Moses, or to any of a multitude of other people whose life stories are told in Scripture. Jesus' words are true of every believer who has ever lived. We get to understand fully only "afterwards".

That was especially true for Joseph. Placed in a pit by his brothers, sold into slavery in Egypt, falsely accused by Captain Potiphar's wife, unjustly imprisoned, forgotten by Pharaoh's cupbearer—how often he must have asked, even if it were with growing submission, *Lord, what are you doing? Do you still love me? I don't understand you.* Eventually he saw that the Lord was working in his own life: for 14 years teaching him patience in order to train him to exercise it for the next fourteen years. But Joseph also realised that God was working in the lives of his father and brothers to undo the consequences of their sin and jealousy. What was intended to harm him was, in the hands of the Lord, meant for good.

The same could be said of Naomi. Sadness upon sadness seemed to punctuate her life: emigration from the only land in which God had promised blessing; the death of her husband, Elimelech, and then of her two sons, Mahlon and Kilion.

Yet these events would lead to the conversion of her daughter-in-law Ruth (Ruth 1 v 16-17 is more than nice wording for a wedding service!). And that in turn led to Ruth's marriage to Boaz, and the birth of their son, Obed.

But even Naomi knew "only in part". She was never able to read the closing verses of the book of Ruth, where we learn what God had planned for *afterwards*. If Naomi had asked the question, *Why has life been so bitter?* it was not fully answered in Ruth's marriage and child-bearing. No, the answer to that question is not to be found until the last word of the book, which records the final name in the Ruth-Boaz family tree: *David* (4 v 22).

Yes, God's purpose was bigger and more far-sighted than the birth of Obed. He had the birth of King David in mind.

But that's not all. The family tree in Ruth 4 v 18-22 reappears in Matthew 1 v 1-17, in the genealogy that begins Matthew's Christmas account: "and Boaz the father of Obed by Ruth, and Obed the father of Jesse, and Jesse the father of David the king … and Jacob the father of Joseph the husband of Mary, *of whom Jesus was born, who is called Christ*" (v 5-6, 16). Here, then, is the ultimate answer to Naomi's *Lord, what are you doing in my life?* God was getting things ready for Jesus!

Everything in the Bible points us to this. We can see the same pattern in the life of Joseph. He did not know all the "good" that God was intending when he was sold as a slave into Egypt. Did he understand enough to think that it might have something to do with God's covenant with Abraham? Might Egypt be the land God had in view when he promised "your offspring will be sojourners in a land that is not theirs and will be servants there, and they will be afflicted for four hundred years. But … they shall come out … And they shall come back here" (Genesis 15 v 13-16)?

But even if Joseph grasped that, he knew little of how God's purposes would finally be fulfilled in the incarnation, when the ultimate seed of Abraham, Jesus Christ, would bruise the head of the serpent (12 v 3; 3 v 15; Galatians 3 v 16; Revelation 12 v 1-17).

What the Lord said to Peter he could have said to both Joseph and Naomi: "What I am doing you do not understand now, but afterwards you will understand" (John 13 v 7). For Joseph, Naomi, and Peter there was an "afterwards".

The same is true for us, as Paul says here: "Now I know in part; then I shall know fully" (1 Corinthians 13 v 12). Perhaps, as you look back at the end of another year, you find yourself asking, "Lord, what are you doing?" It might be that you can see glimpses of the good that he is doing—you know his purposes "in part". But take comfort in the thought that one day, when you look back on your life from the vantage point of eternity, you will know fully. You will at last see the details of your life in the context of God's grand narrative.

But Paul adds something that we may too easily ignore—something that gives Christians great comfort. At the moment we only partially understand the Lord and his ways. But here is our assurance and solace: he knows us fully and perfectly: "I have been fully known".

If non-believers think about this seriously, it terrifies them. We can hide nothing from the Lord. Our hearts are like an open book before him (Hebrews 4 v 12-13). But what terrifies the unbeliever is a comfort to the believer. Everything about us is already known to our Lord. That is why so many Christians have loved the words of the Heidelberg Catechism:

Question 1: What is your only comfort in life and death?

Answer: That I with body and soul, both in life and death, am not my own, but belong to my faithful Saviour Jesus Christ; who, with his precious blood, has fully satisfied for all my sins, and delivered me from all the power of the devil; and so preserves me that without the will of my heavenly Father, not a hair can fall from my head; yes, that all things must be subservient to my salvation, and therefore, by his Holy Spirit, he also assures me of eternal life, and makes me sincerely willing and ready, henceforth, to live unto him.

How can we be so sure? Because the One who knows us is the One who loves us. He is the One whose hand was on Joseph's life, whose love guarded Naomi through her darkest days, who stooped down to wash Simon Peter's dirty feet. So we can wait patiently until "afterwards", since we know we are loved by the One who knows everything about us, and who will love us "to the end" (John 13 v 1).

REFLECTION

"Lord, what are you doing?" When have you asked that question in the past year? Why is it a comfort to know that you "have been fully known" by God?

PRAYER

Alone with none but thee, my God,
I journey on my way.
What need I fear when thou art near,
O King of night and day?
More safe am I within thy hand
Than if a host should round me stand.

My destined time is known to thee,
And death will keep his hour;
Did warriors strong around me throng,
They could not stay his power:
No walls of stone can man defend
When thou thy messenger dost send.

The child of God can fear no ill,
His chosen dread no foe;
We leave our fate with thee, and wait
Thy bidding when to go.
'Tis not from chance our comfort springs
Thou art our trust, O King of kings.
Attributed to Columba (521-597)

23. "THE WELL-KNOWN THREE"

So now faith, hope, and love abide, these three…

1 Corinthians 13 v 13

My New Testament professor used to refer to faith, hope, and love as "the well-known three". It is an apt description. They roll off the tongue together. But they do so largely, if not exclusively, because of the apostle Paul.

Paul refers to this trio another half dozen times in his letters. He writes to the Thessalonians about their "work of faith and labour of love and steadfastness of hope in our Lord Jesus Christ" (1 Thessalonians 1 v 3). These were the tell-tale signs of authentic Christianity that assured him the Thessalonians were the real deal. Without them they would not last in the heat of the battle, for they needed "the breastplate of faith and love, and for a helmet the hope of salvation" (5 v 8).

The same was true of the Colossians. Paul had never met them. So how could he be sure they had really become Christians? He tells us the answer: "We heard of your faith in Christ Jesus and of the love that you have ... because of the hope laid up for you in heaven" (Colossians 1 v 4-5).

But why do "the well-known three" of faith, hope and love belong together?

Paul's fullest explanation is to be found in Romans 5 v 1-11. It is a remarkable passage, held together by the threefold refrain "we rejoice in" or "exult in", which occurs in a kind of ascending sequence of statements:

• We rejoice in hope of the glory of God (v 2).

Not only that, but...

• We rejoice in our sufferings (v 3).

Even more than that...

• We also rejoice in God (v 11).

There is an internal logic to the steps in Paul's argument. His reasoning is not difficult to follow.

The person who knows that they have been justified by faith and have peace with God also knows they are destined to experience the glory of God in heaven. There they will see Christ face to face and be made like him (1 John 3 v 2; 2 Corinthians 3 v 18). And there they will be able to worship Father, Son, and Holy Spirit without sin and without end. They therefore rejoice in this hope (Romans 5 v 2). Even an unbeliever can understand that. Such a situation, if it is real, is enviable indeed.

But Paul says there is more: "*More than that*, we rejoice in our sufferings". If the first step of joy on which we stand is *enviable*, this next one is, surely, *remarkable*.

Rejoicing in sufferings? Paul has taken a step down, as it were, (from the hope of glory to the experience of

Love Came Down at Christmas

suffering) and turned it into a step up! How can this be true? Of course, he is not saying that Christians enjoy pain; we are not masochists. Rather, the gospel teaches us that God has a purpose in our sufferings—he works in us through them. Our sufferings become the raw materials out of which he forges glory: "Suffering *produces* endurance, and endurance *produces* character, and character *produces* hope" (v 3-4). But what hope? Hope in the glory of God, of course! We rejoice in our sufferings because we know that through them God is doing something transformative in our lives. He is putting glory into us.

But we have all tasted disappointed hopes. Perhaps at this time of year you feel them more keenly than ever. So how can we be sure that this hope—the hope of glory—won't be disappointed? Paul tells us how: this "hope does not put us to shame [or 'disappoint us', NIV1984] because God's love has been poured into our hearts through the Holy Spirit who has been given to us" (v 5).

What does this mean? Simply this: the Christian can be sure their hope will never disappoint them because they already enjoy a foretaste of its realisation. Heaven, as Jonathan Edwards noted, is "a world of love". But it is as though God has punctured a small hole in the floor of heaven through which the Spirit pours into our hearts a little taste of that heavenly love here and now. The Christian senses him or herself to be loved. As someone once expressed it to me, "When I came to Christ, I felt loved for the first time in my life!"

It is because of the nature of this love that Paul can take a third step and say, *More than that, we rejoice in God himself.* If rejoicing in the hope of glory is, even to the non-Christian, *enviable*, and rejoicing in suffering is *remarkable*, then, surely, rejoicing in God himself is virtually *incomprehensible.*

It is inconceivable to the unbeliever how the first question and answer of the Westminster Shorter Catechism works:

Question 1: What is the chief end of man? [That is, what is the point of our existence?]

Answer: Man's chief end is to glorify God, and to enjoy him for ever.

Why do those who do not know the Lord find this so difficult to understand? Because they see God as the spoiler of their pleasure; for them, glorifying him would be a recipe for losing control of their own lives. The truth is, however, that there is no lasting enjoyment without this enjoyment of God. And without it we can never find ourselves and our true destiny. For we were made by God, as his image, for loving fellowship with him. John Newton was right when he penned his hymn "Glorious things of thee are spoken":

Solid joys and lasting treasures,
None but Zion's children know.

But the question inevitably arises: how can we be sure? The answer? God has demonstrated his love for us. He has proved it: "God shows his love for us in that while we were still sinners [and ungodly and enemies], *Christ died for us*" (v 8).

Ultimately, this is why "the well-known three" belong together. Faith in Christ leads to the hope of glory. That hope is anchored in God's love for us in Christ. Our love is simply the overflow of the love he has poured out into our hearts by the Holy Spirit.

Thank God for that love! It comes down to us now through the Holy Spirit only because, first of all, in the incarnation of the Son of God, that *Love came down at Christmas*.

REFLECTION

God's love has been poured into your heart. How will that be expressed in faith, hope and love in your life this Christmas?

PRAYER

O God,
whose blessed Son was manifested that he might
destroy the works of the devil,
and make us the sons of God,
and heirs of eternal life;
grant us, we beseech thee, that,
having this hope, we may purify ourselves,
even as he is pure;

that when he shall appear again
with power and great glory,
we may be made like unto him
in his eternal and glorious kingdom;
where with thee, O Father, and thee, O Holy Ghost,
he liveth and reigneth, ever one God,
world without end. Amen.

The Book of Common Prayer

24. THE GREATEST

But the greatest of these is love.

1 Corinthians 13 v 13

Everyone agrees. Faith is admirable, hope is wonderful, but love is the greatest. There are songs about faith and words about hope, but the songs and words about love easily surpass them in number and in eloquence.

But why is love the greatest? Is it just because Paul says so here?

On Christmas Day this year, as every year, some TV channel will show a rerun of one or other of the movie versions of Charles Dickens' *A Christmas Carol*. It is a quintessentially Dickensian novel, and has given the English language one of its most memorable nouns— "scrooge". The story touches something deep within us because of the way it describes the transformation of a mean and miserly heart into one of sympathy and love.

But if we want to learn what Christmas means, and about the meaning of love, we would be wiser to read someone who was an almost exact contemporary of Dickens: Sir James Young Simpson (1811-1870).

James Young Simpson was born in Bathgate in central Scotland. From his early days he seemed destined for a stellar career. A brilliant student, he completed his final medical exams at the age of eighteen, and had to wait another three years before he could graduate. His accomplishments over his lifetime were such that the day of his funeral was declared a holiday, and it is said that 100,000 people lined the streets of Edinburgh on the way to Warriston cemetery, where he was buried (the family having declined Westminster Abbey). James Young Simpson is best known today because he was the first surgeon to use chloroform as an anaesthetic (he used to experiment on himself and some friends to test the anaesthetic properties of new chemicals!).

But in his own day, Simpson was also well known because of his Christian faith. He well understood why Paul wrote that love is "the greatest", because he understood the gospel.

He explained it very simply in a little essay entitled *My Substitute*:

> *When I was a boy at school, I saw a sight I never can forget—a man tied to a cart, dragged before the people's eyes through the streets of my native town, his back torn and bleeding from the lash.*
>
> *It was a shameful punishment. For* many *offences? No, for one offence. Did any of the townsmen offer to divide the lashes with him? No, he who committed the offence bore the penalty all alone. It was the penalty*

of a changing human law, for it was the last instance of its infliction.

When I was a student at the university, I saw another sight I never can forget—a man brought out to die. His arms were pinioned, his face was already as pale as death, thousands of eager eyes were on him as he came up from the jail in sight. Did any man ask to die in his room? Did any friend come and loose the ropes and say, "Put it around my neck, I will die instead"? No, he underwent the sentence of the law. For many *offences? No, for one offence. He had stolen a money parcel from a stage-coach. He broke the law at one point, and died for it. It was the penalty of a changing human law in this case also. It was the last instance of capital punishment being inflicted for that offence.*

I saw another sight, it matters not when—myself a sinner standing on the brink of ruin, deserving nought but hell. For one *sin? No, for many, many sins committed against the unchanging laws of God. But again, I looked and saw Jesus, my Substitute, scourged in my stead, and dying on the cross for me. I looked, and wept, and was forgiven. And it seemed to me to be my duty to tell you of that Saviour, to see if you will not also "look and live".*

And how simple it all becomes when God opens the eye. A friend who lately came from Paris told me of an English groom there, a very careless old man,

*who had during a severe illness been made to feel
that he was a sinner. He dared not die as he was.
The clergyman whom he sent for got tired of visiting
him, having told him all he then knew of the way
of salvation. But one Sunday afternoon the groom's
daughter waited in the vestry after church, saying
"You must come once more, sir; I cannot see my
father again without you." "I can tell him nothing
new," said the preacher; "but I may take the sermon
I have been preaching and read it to him."*

*The dying man lay as before in anguish, thinking
of his sins, and whither they must carry him. "My
friend, I have come to read to you the sermon I have
just preached. First, I shall tell you of the text:
'He was wounded for our transgressions' (Isaiah 53
v 5). Now I shall read." "Hold!" said the dying
man. "I have it! Read no more. He was wounded
for* my *transgressions." Soon after he died rejoicing
in Christ.*

In the incarnation the Son of God became "a man of
sorrows, and acquainted with grief" (Isaiah 53 v 3). But
we are not justified, or adopted into God's family, or
sanctified, or glorified simply because the Son of God
shared our flesh and our sorrows. Yes, that means he
can sympathise with us in our weakness because he experienced it. But he came to accomplish much more—
something we could never do for ourselves—he came
to die for us. Only when we can say, "He was wounded

for our transgressions" have we grasped the meaning of the gospel and the wonder of love.

This is the heart of the matter—as Sir James Young Simpson saw so clearly. This is what we should never forget on Christmas Eve and on Christmas Day. The Son of God was born for us in order to die for us. When we see that, then we have begun to understand Love. And then we discover the joyful truth of John Donne's words:

> *Whom God loves, he loves to the end:*
> *And not to their end, and to their death,*
> *But to his end.*
> *And his end is that he might love them more.*

For this reason, *Love came down at Christmas.*

REFLECTION
Read back over the whole of 1 Corinthians 13. Which description of love have you been particularly struck by? What difference does it make to know that this is how Christ has loved you?

PRAYER
> *O Lord, holy and true, who opens and none can shut,*
> *as you have set before your church an open door,*
> *strengthen your servants boldly to enter in*
> *and to declare your name,*
> *that they who oppose may yet come to worship*

and may know that you love your church.
Grant to your people patience to keep your word,
and keep them from the hour of trial which is coming
upon the whole world to try them who dwell on the earth.
And encourage all Christians in every land
to hold fast that which you have given,
that the crown of glory be not taken away,
but that having overcome, they may stand before you
as pillars in the temple of God
and bear the name of the heavenly city
and your own new name, O Christ our God.
Father, we commend to you all who are joined to us
by natural bonds of love;
the little children dear to our hearts,
and all who for our sakes daily deny themselves.
May all our kindred,
having your Holy Spirit as their helper,
be at peace and have unfeigned love among themselves.
And grant them, O Lord, not only sufficient to supply
the needs of this present life but also the good and
eternal gifts that are laid up for them who do your
commandments.
Through the same Jesus Christ, our Lord. Amen.
Columba (521-597)

ENJOY GOD'S LOVE IN EVERY MOMENT

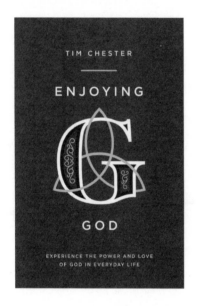

We believe in God, we serve God, we trust God, but would we say that we experience God on a day to day basis? This seminal work by Tim Chester looks at what a relationship with God looks like and how it is possible. As we see how the three persons of the Trinity relate to us in our day-to-day lives and how to respond, we will discover the key to enjoying God in every moment of everyday.

thegoodbook.co.uk | .com

COMPANY

BIBLICAL | RELEVANT | ACCESSIBLE

At The Good Book Company, we are dedicated to helping Christians and local churches grow. We believe that God's growth process always starts with hearing clearly what he has said to us through his timeless word—the Bible.

Ever since we opened our doors in 1991, we have been striving to produce Bible-based resources that bring glory to God. We have grown to become an international provider of user-friendly resources to the Christian community, with believers of all backgrounds and denominations using our books, Bible studies, devotionals, evangelistic resources, and DVD-based courses.

We want to equip ordinary Christians to live for Christ day by day, and churches to grow in their knowledge of God, their love for one another, and the effectiveness of their outreach.

Call us for a discussion of your needs or visit one of our local websites for more information on the resources and services we provide.

Your friends at The Good Book Company

thegoodbook.com | thegoodbook.co.uk
thegoodbook.com.au | thegoodbook.co.nz
thegoodbook.co.in